THE BEST NEW CRICKET WRITING
The New Ball

THE BEST NEW CRICKET WRITING

The New Ball

VOLUME ONE

England v
Australia

EDITED BY ROB STEEN

TWO HEADS
PUBLISHING

First published in 1998 by
Two Heads Publishing
9 Whitehall Park
London
N19 3TS

ISBN 1 897850 83 2

Cover spine quotes:
Graham Dilley to Ian Botham, Headingley 1981. Greg Matthews

Cover and Book Design by Lance Bellers
Cover Photographs by Mark Ray

Printed and bound in the UK by Biddles, Guildford

Contents

A Nice Little Urner

ACKNOWLEDGEMENTS

Muchos gracias to all the spiffing contributors for their willingness,
punctuality and top-bloody-holeness; to my one-in-a-million
publisher Charles Frewin, for giving birth to such a bouncy brainchild;
to designer Lance Bellers for his boundless energy and creativity;
to Mike Marqusee, Huw Richards and Sportspages for advice and
encouragement; to Todd Rundgren, Neil Hannon, Kelsey Grammer,
Ally Brown, Sammy Sosa, the New York Mets and the Chicago
Cubs for sustenance; to Jeremy Novick (he'll know why); to the fair
Anne for nodding with something vaguely akin to enthusiasm
whenever I waved a proof of the cover under her nose; to Laura,
Josef and Evie for being.

Editor's Note

I know, I know. Just what the world needs. Another pillage of the rainforests in the name of the planet's most time-consuming, least obviously exhilarating ball game. Fortunately, I believe I can claim without too much fear of contradiction that The New Ball is both a unique and worthy addition to the proud traditions of cricket literature.

Published twice a year, at the start and end of each English season, the purpose of The New Ball is twofold. Firstly, to fill the void between the press (magazines and newspapers) and more traditional books; secondly, to provide a forum for writers – and photographers – to paint pictures, examine issues and develop ideas that might otherwise struggle to find a fitting platform.

My declaration of principles may not quite match Charles Foster Kane's for length or substance, but suffice to say that only the original and the passionate need apply. At a time when this hitherto archly-conservative game of ours is showing promising signs of radicalism, the expression and exchange of views is imperative. The plonkers need prodding, so let's prod. During its passionate but all-too brief existence, Inside Edge magazine went some of the way towards fulfilling these objectives: a lap dancer, if you will. Like Cynthia Payne, The New Ball will go all the way – and then some.

To my delight, the response has been overwhelming, both in enthusiasm and quality. Any manager fortunate enough to be able to assemble a team boasting the diverse talents of Berry, Brenkley, Engel, Haigh, Hedgcock, Ray and Steel, not to mention a couple of useful ringers in Chappell (I) and Wellham, cannot possibly complain that life is shortchanging him. I am confident you will concur with this ludicrously biased assertion.

All that said, you may have noticed that Volume One has more than a touch of the retros about it. (Volume Two, due out shortly before next year's World Cup, will establish the template proper, focusing on the game in broader, more progressive terms: from east to west, from north to south, from schools to globalisation, from the here to the now.) Given the nature of this winter's festivities Down Under, apologies are most definitely reserved. What better way to kick off this celebration of an addiction than to pay tribute to its most celebrated contest?

In order for this Pom to achieve something approximating to a semblance of balance, I have endeavoured to instil a degree of reciprocity: Murray Hedgcock on why, despite living in London for 25 years, he so miserably fails the Tebbit Test, Martin Johnson on why Australians infiltrate his nasal passages; Gideon Haigh on the tragic magic of Jack Iverson, Stephen Brenkley on the similarly meteoric Frank Tyson. There are also fresh ruminations on history: Scyld Berry digs back to 1894-95, to the first truly great Ashes series – the first to span five Tests, the torch that lit the bonfire; Mark Steel analyses the state of Australia at the time of Bodyline; Matthew Engel recalls his maiden Antipodean jaunt as correspondent of *The Guardian*. And then there are the less, shall we say, pigeonholeable items: Dirk Wellham delves into the sexual politics of the Australian dressing room, Barton Funk reveals some rum doings half a century hence, and Ian Chappell unmasks his favourite Pom. Something for everyone – a carnival tonight.

I WOULD ALSO like to take this opportunity to throw the field open. If you have a hankering to compose a 5,000-word article on a matter of cricketing significance – be it a profile, an interview, a piece of investigative journalism, a rant or even a story – please feel free to throw ideas my way. While declining responsibility for unsolicited manuscripts, and warning any takers that issues are planned up to six months in advance (and thematically at that), I can assure you that anything sent will be read – and anything published paid for. Tip 1: think left-field and lateral. Tip 2: the angrier the bees – and the bigger the bonnet – the better. Tip 3: avoid poetry, misty-eyed reminiscences and spiffing tales of the village green.

It was Mickey/Micky Stewart (I'm never quite sure how the erstwhile England manager wishes us to spell his forename these days) who famously urged his fast bowlers to treat a new ball like a bride. I trust that this particular fresh cherry will be consumed without any such tentativeness. Read it and reap.

Rob Steen
Alexandra Palace
November 1998
E-mail: Robsteen@compuserve.com

NB *Eagle-eyed students of the game should note that unless otherwise stated, all facts appearing alongside page numbers (as per the one at the foot of this page) relate strictly to Tests between England and Australia where the urn was at stake; correct to the start of the 1998-99 series.*

Mark Ray was born in 1952.
A photographer at heart and a
cricket writer by profession, he
has covered tours to England,
South Africa, New Zealand and
Pakistan and has published,
amongst others, a book of
cricket photojournalism. Apart
from Australian Rules, he is not
particularly interested in sport.
Cricket, of course, is different.

**Favourite Ashes bowling
performance**
Bob Massie's Test debut, Lord's
1972. He took 8-84 and 8-53 and
bent the ball in the air like a
magician. A brief burst of genius.

**The Cobbers repeatedly
pummel the Poms
because...** the Poms play too
much meaningless cricket and so
lack passion. The Cobbers are not
afraid to pursue excellence while
the Poms cannot condescend to
self-improvement.

Mark Ray

Three Lions and a Tiger: An Ashes Gallery

WG GRACE LORD'S MUSEUM, JUNE 1989

SHANE WARNE ADELAIDE OVAL, JANUARY 1994

Rob Steen
Timeless Tests

Rob Steen is an allegedly acclaimed author, inveterate freelance journalist and unabashed Londoner. Last time he checked he was covering cricket for *The Guardian*, the *Sunday Telegraph* and the *Financial Times*. His greatest ambition, other than to see at least one of his daughters marry a Microsoft chairman, is to stage a Test match in New York. His favourite word is maverick.

Favourite Ashes innings
Phil DeFreitas's 88 at Adelaide, 1995. A matchwinner conjured out of thin air and a V-sign from a bloke blamed far too often for the shortcomings of others.

England finish second so often because... flying the flag in an increasingly diverse multi-cultural society means less than paying the mortgage.

As the actress doubtless said to the bishop at some juncture or other, is this all going to end in the first scene or will I get the full five acts? As a loyal but over-demanding Pom, it was the question uppermost in my teenybopper mind at the outset of every Test match: will it go the distance?

The principal reason for this was quite simple: I couldn't get enough cricket. The longer a game went on, the happier I was. Same with footie. I willed Benfica to equalise in the 1968 European Cup final. Of course I wanted those other Old Traffordians to win, but I craved extra-time more. And just think: if Jaime Graca hadn't knocked one in at the far post with 11 minutes to go, the world would have been denied George Best's sublime second goal, the most outrageously arrogant act perpetrated by a citizen of the United Kingdom on a field of play. As the first-class counties seldom tire of reminding us, never mind the quality, feel the quantity.

As the years went by the question modified. Can a Test sustain interest over and above partiality and prayer, beyond bias and blinkers? Could the plot shifts and protracted dramatics transcend the outcome? Yes, yes and thrice yes. Happy endings are unnecessary. Not only can the longeurs be worth tolerating, they allow contemplation, regeneration, anticipation. The beauty can be in the stillness, in the suspension of time.

In recent Anglo-Antipodean history, unfortunately, Tests capable of that degree of stimulation – let alone the common or garden, honest-to-goodness, goose-bumping, cuticle-crunching cracker – have been almost as thin on the ground as sun terraces in Greenland. In fact, you have to go back to Sydney '87, to those soppy old days when Thatcherotops and Reaganosaurus Rex roamed the earth, to locate the last Ashes encounter entering its fifth day with both sides scenting the spoils, nostrils equally aflare. The aesthete and the neutral have suffered every bit as grievously as the Englishman. Fortunately, I'm sufficiently lengthy of tooth to be able to recall a time when the words "Australia", "beat" and "England" did not habitually occupy sentences in the same order.

It will be noted, nonetheless, that the following entirely personal Top Ten includes just two Australian victories. There is a sound excuse for this other than incurable myopia. For some inexplicable reason, the Cobbers usually bottle the close ones. On the four occasions over the last 70 years that Tests between the two have been decided by fewer than 20 runs, the Poms have won the lot. Of the four occasions that they have ever been decided by a margin of two wickets or fewer, the Poms have prevailed in three. Proof of steelier minds? Right, and Michael Caine's a Belgian.

Composing anally-retentive lists of this nature is usually a bit of a con. The very longevity of this particular fixture means that the lister will always trumpet battles fought long before they were so much as a mischievous glint in their mother's eye. Distance lends mystique. Who could forget that 1902 epic at Old Trafford? Or that encore at The Oval a fortnight later? Or Benaud's match at Manchester in '61? Yet without that sense of participation, of living with the ebb and flow – at however many removes – the one essential will always be missing. Feeling the rush as it happens, experiencing that nightly pause and morning tingle: these are the passports to everlasting love. Try as it might, a scorecard can only jog a memory. It cannot create one.

Besides the stipulation that the match should have taken place sometime over the past three decades (I was 10 at the time of my initial close encounter in 1968), there is one other pre-requisite: all candidates should be competitive for at least half their duration. Which rules out Headingley '81: Australia, after all, took the first 11 sessions. The kamikaze efforts of the home order on the last afternoon (well, they had regained the urn) also rules out Adelaide

'95, much as it went deep into the final hour. Ditto, for similar reasons, Edgbaston '97, where Australia's Sunday slither transformed a humdinger into a premature ejaculator.

And so, after much rewinding of videos, to the nominees. Included are the means (newspapers aside) by which I followed each one's progress. Purely in the interests of honesty.

THE OVAL 1968
Means: Radio on beach in Devon; Ferguson b&w portable.
Scores: England 494 (Edrich 164, D'Oliveira 158) and 181 (Connolly 4-65); Australia 324 (Lawry 135) and 125 (Underwood 7-50) ENGLAND won by 226 runs
Material impact on destination of urn: None.

THE MOST far-reaching five days in the history of the ball? Quite possibly. Had wicketkeeper Barry Jarman accepted a relatively straightforward offering from Basil D'Oliveira when the latter had made 31 of his eventual 158, John Vorster would never had had cause to denounce the MCC party to tour South Africa as "the team of the anti-apartheid movement", the sports boycott might never have happened and Nelson Mandela might still be residing on Robben Island. Come to think of it, if just one of the half-dozen lives Dolly enjoyed during that knock had been withheld, Sir Alec Douglas-Home, the Home Office and the MCC would have been spared a goodly dose of richly-deserved embarrassment. Which is just as well.

And then there were those heroic broom-and-blanket wielders who helped mop up on the last afternoon after a deluge of 40 days' and nights' intensity. Here, for once, was a day to be grateful for rain. Without it the match would almost certainly have been over with a couple of hours to spare, coitus fatally interrupted.

Thanks in no small measure to D'Oliveira, England recovered from 113 for three on the first day, quadrupling their score. Urn retained, Australia replied by losing their first wicket at seven, relaxed as Bill Lawry and Ian Redpath added 129, whereupon the next five went for 52. The follow-on was still 25 runs distant when Lawry became the eighth to go at the outset of day four. Step forward the improbable Horatio, debutant off-spinner Ashley Mallett: never would the skinny South Australian top that unbeaten 43 in his subsequent 49 innings under the baggy green.

By now only four complete sessions remained, obliging the home batsmen, for arguably the only time in a decade of attrition and caution, to mount a collective assault in an Ashes Test. There was a series to be squared, pride to be reclaimed. Colin Milburn hooked Graham McKenzie for four and pulled Alan Connolly for six, the lead doubled at a run a minute. Even more admirably, Lawry declined to slow things down, his men wheeling down 58-and-a-bit overs. The target was 352, the draw the aim once the Victorian openers had been dispatched in quick succession before stumps, Lawry for the second time that day. Having refused to budge for the previous three-and-a-half sessions it was the very least the stubborn old coot could do.

Yet what endures most from that gripping last day is not so much Underwood's consummate guile and control on a helpful pitch, nor John Inverarity's skilful stoicism, nor even the sight of 10 Englishmen crouched around the bat like expectant fathers. Picture this instead. With 10 minutes left, Underwood does for Johnny Gleeson, Australia's No.10, bowled misjudging the line. Mounting his bike, victim smiles warmly at vanquisher, seemingly happy that justice is about to be done. Then pats him on the derriere. Right there in front of God, Jim Swanton and everything. One for the cockles.

Key moment: Jarman plays no stroke on the final evening as D'Oliveira – who else – clips his off-bail.
Sound bite: "Don't bother to look at the television. I shall make a hundred all right." (D'Oliveira to Her Indoors)

SYDNEY 1971
Means: Under blanket with father's crusty, crackly transistor radio; brief b&w TV highlights.
Scores: England 184 (Illingworth 42) and 302 (Luckhurst 59); Australia 264 (G Chappell 65) and 160 (Stackpole 67). ENGLAND won by 62 runs.
Material impact: England regain Ashes.

THE ONLY seventh Test in history was done and dusted before lunch on the final day, but no matter. It was violent, ill-tempered and at times downright ugly, but we can forgive that just this once. The urn was on the line, Ian Chappell and Ray Illingworth were going head-to-head as opposing captains for the first time, and England squeezed home without their most lethal weapons, Geoff Boycott and John Snow. All in all, there was enough dynamite to blow up the Opera House and still have some left over for the bridge.

Let's dispense with the nasty stuff first. When Terry Jenner was felled by a short-pitcher from Snow, the ensuing unpleasantries between Illingworth and the umpires over what did or did not constitute intimidation prompted the crowd to howl their protests and England to flee the field. They returned when their captain was reminded that the opposition would be awarded victory if he didn't get back out there sharpish. The Sussex poet got his comeuppance via a drunken punter and a picket fence.

In contrast to every other chapter of the series, the ball reigned throughout, as so often seems to be the case when the game reaches its apogee of expression. There were no century stands; nobody reached 70. Keith Stackpole's bullish counter-attack on the penultimate evening was the sole exception to widespread subservience. Better yet, the balance between speed and spin was well-nigh perfect: Lillee, Dell, Snow, Lever and Willis collected 18 victims between them, ditto Jenner, O'Keeffe, Illingworth and Underwood. There was also a scalp apiece for one-cap wonder Ken Eastwood (who bowled as many overs with his extremely occasional leggies – five – as he scored runs) and those dukes of the dibbly-dobbly, D'Oliveira and Doug Walters. Was a pitch ever quite so wondrously democratic? Hell, even Keith Fletcher had a dart.

The deciding factor, nonetheless, was the untrammeled self-belief of The Artist Henceforth To Be Known As Illytollah. On the last day, or so the pundits assured him, pace was the answer, with or without Snow. Illy knew better. Opening up with himself and Underwood, he held fast as his partner faltered, making the critical breach and ultimately being chaired off the field having joined Jardine as the only England captain this century to retrieve the urn Down Under. Even Devon Malcolm might have given him a kiss.

The New Ball

Key moment: Greg Chappell lured by Illy, stumped by Alan Knott. *Sound bite:* "He gave me the feeling we could win under his leadership in any situation." (Knotty on Illy)

THE OVAL 1972
Means: Second day in flesh; rest on TV in between back-garden Tests. *Scores:* England 284 (Knott 92, Lillee 5-58) and 356 (Wood 90, Lillee 5-123); Australia 399 (I Chappell 118, G Chappell 113, Edwards 79, Underwood 4-90) and 242-5 (Stackpole 79). AUSTRALIA won by five wickets. *Material impact:* None.

THE LAST six-day Test in Blighty and the first hint of the swagger of the Chappell era. Confounded by Underwood and fuserium at Headingley, Australia came to Kennington thoroughly miffed and 2-1 down in the rubber, prime objective thwarted. Ian Chappell's pre-match bonding session did the trick, however, and Lillee, Marsh and Vic Richardson's grandsons, the cornerstones of the new order, ensured a just result.

The freeze-frames are endless. Unfortunately for this teenage Pom, most of them featured Lillee rumbling in from the Vauxhall Road end, elbows wagging, 'tache twitching, every stride a snarl, bats no more than shields. Only Knott and Barry Wood had the *cojones* to unsheath their swords. Then there were the Chappells. I thought I'd lucked out: my inaugural day of Ashes warfare was the Friday. With England's first innings already wrapped up, I would be spared the pain of monitoring each ball with heart in mouth. Seeing the brothers put on 201 wasn't that much of an improvement, but at least there was Greg's magisterial elegance to relish. By the time I got back to the Northern Line I felt doubly disloyal. Not even Tom Graveney could have been *that* good.

Yet England clawed their way back, setting a daunting target, and might well have won had Illingworth not been stricken on the fourth evening, turning his ankle over in the footmarks. With Snow nursing an arm clattered by Lillee and D'Oliveira also unable to bowl, the attack was now a trio.

Chappelli and Stackpole sailed the ship more than halfway home but then both they and Ross Edwards were washed overboard in the space of five runs. Chappell Minor followed at 171 – 71 to get, the new ball fresh and a less-than seaworthy tail all but exposed. Paul Sheahan, though, remained serene, Rod Marsh clambered aboard with cutlass in teeth and the most two-sided Ashes debate of the past 60 years sped to its rightful denouement.

Key moment: Marsh's blitzkrieg against the new ball.
Sound bite: "If we go home two-all it's been a successful tour. If we go home 3-1 down we'll be looked on as failures." (Chappelli to troops)

LORD'S 1975
Means: World Service on kibbutz.
Scores: England 315 (Greig 96, Lillee 4-84) and 436-7 declared (Edrich 175); Australia 268 (Edwards 99, Lillee 73, Snow 4-66) and 329-3 (I Chappell 86, McCosker 79, G Chappell 73*). DRAWN
Material impact: None.

ALL RIGHT, the pitch flattened out into the most boring strip this side of John Major doing the Full Monty. Granted, 484 in a smidgin under even time is not the most enticing gauntlet ever flung down. For disciples of the even contest, however, here were riches untold.

Battered to oblivion Down Under less than four months previously, England were already a defeat and a captain down, Mike Denness having resigned following criticism of his unfortunate insertion at Edgbaston, his side all too easily unglued on the last sticky wicket seen on English soil. Yet lo and behold, for the first time in 14 innings against Lillee and Thomson, a specialist English batsman made a hundred (over the previous 13 they'd only managed six half-Montys). The spell had been broken.

The gems, nevertheless, were reserved for the first two days. Lillee removing the first four with the ruthless ease of a cheese slicer; David Steele polishing his glasses, wrapping a towel round his left thigh and plodding out to halt the panic, Captain Mainwaring incarnate –

and getting lost in the gents; Tony Greig, Denness's successor, launching the riposte, abetted by Knott; Snow making short work of the Chappells as Australia slip to 81 for seven; Ross Edwards proving once and for all that he could bat as annoyingly as he patrolled the covers; Lillee's rousing unorthodoxies keeping the deficit down to manageable proportions. The first five wickets in each innings combined for 201 runs, the last five, 382. One spectator passed eloquent comment on the remainder by treating HQ to its maiden streak. Only half-great – but what a half!

Key moment: Steele pulling his third ball from Lillee for four.
Sound bite: "Who is this guy? Groucho Marx?" (Thommo meets Steele)

EDGBASTON 1981
Means: Sony 12-inch and BT phone line (glimpses sneaked during fictitious duties for local estate agents, scores checked every 15 minutes on 162); girlfriend's bed.
Scores: England 189 (Brearley 48, Alderman 5-42) and 219 (Bright 5-68); Australia 258 (Hughes 47, Emburey 4-43) and 121 (Border 40, Botham 5-11). ENGLAND won by 29 runs.
Material impact: England go 2-1 up; retain Ashes in next game.

ANOTHER DAYMARE for the batters. For the first time in 46 years and 668 Tests, not a soul reached 50, but who cared? Headingley may have stirred the imagination, but this four-day masterpiece offered suspense on a positively Hitchcockian scale.

Series pegged level after three, England were out well before the close on day one, Mike Brearley alone sticking around for more than an hour and a half on a surface that could have taught a slug a few things about sluggishness. A mood of unaccountable recklessness (Headingley hype, perhaps?) played squarely into the hands of Lillee, Terry Alderman and that theoretically slow but really-rather-brisk left-armer Ray Bright. "They found ways of getting out which are unlikely to figure prominently in their autobiographies," opined Michael Melford in the *Daily Telegraph*.

Rackemann came in trailing only slightly more pretensions to authentic batsmanship than a platypus

The New Ball

Underpinned by Graeme Wood and raised to occasional heights by the more dashing blades of Kim Hughes and Martin Kent, Australia took the lead with five wickets in hand only to stumble once John Emburey had spun one sharply to bowl Graeme Yallop. Still, a potentially priceless advantage of 69 was earned and quickly enhanced, Lillee sending back Brearley with the arrears barely touched. Even more disconcertingly for the disgruntled gathering, the delivery, banged in short, elected to burp rather than bounce.

Not until Bob Taylor joined John Emburey on the Saturday afternoon did England rally for long, the ninth-wicket duo forging their side's only 50 stand. The eventual requirement was 151: eerily reminiscent of Leeds. If only because the pitch was appreciably less spiteful, the Aussies seemed even hotter favourites this time. Recovering from two early strikes by Bob Willis and another by Chris Old, Allan Border and Yallop added 58 in increasing comfort before the latter nicked Emburey to silly point via an involuntary toe. Eighteen runs later, the target below 50, Emburey made one leap, defying a safe response: the ball lobbed from high on the bat to short leg and Mike Gatting hurled it heavenwards. Forty-six minutes and 16 runs later it was all over, Hurricane Botham sweeping up five wickets for one run in 28 balls. One summer, two miracles.

Key moment: Brearley recalls Botham upon Border's exit.
Sound bite: "Give Pete [Willey] a turn." (Botham to Brearley prior to previous over).

MELBOURNE 1982
Means: Under duvet with Walkman and slowly-mending heart.
Scores: England 284 (Tavare 89, Lamb 83, Hogg 4-69, Yardley 4-89) and 294 (Fowler 65, Lawson 4-56); Australia 287 (Hughes 66) and 288 (Hookes 68, Cowans 6-77). DRAWN
Material impact: England cut leeway to 2-1; draw in Sydney secures Ashes for hosts.

HAS ONE man's horror ever turned into a teammate's joy with quite such breathless rapidity? The edge looped towards Chris Tavaré at a nice enough height but slower than England's second slip had bargained for. Cupping both hands towards his chest, he froze as the ball bounced out and up, then somersaulted over his shoulder. His mind blanked. Botham, the bowler, had the look of a fellow primed to dish out some pretty grievous bodily harm.

Geoff Miller had spent the entire series snoozing at first slip: not a sausage had come his way. Now, however, he reacted with alacrity, swooping on the ball as it died then accelerating off the field a-whoopin' an' a-hollerin'. Thus ended the unlikeliest matchwinning stand of all time and the tightest Ashes encounter for 80 years.

The spread-betters would have had a field day with this one. Four completed innings and just 10 runs separating highest and lowest. Beneath shone some dazzling cameos, most notably Tavaré's astounding *volte face* in England's first dig. "Roll up, roll up," you could imagine an Edwardian promoter proclaiming. "See man swap spots for stripes."

Chasing the highest score of the game on a pitch displaying few signs of deterioration bar a modicum of indifferent bounce, Australia began warily, lost their third wicket before lunch on the fourth day then rejoiced as Hughes and Hookes made merry. Then came Norman Cowans, trusted with a lengthy spell for the first time in the series, ripping out Hookes, Marsh and Bruce Yardley in 20 deliveries. Nine were down for 218 when Thomson and Border were conjoined: 37 runs tonight, 37 tomorrow and the job was done. Simple, especially since Willis and his brains trust seemed so reluctant to pressurise Border, setting fields deep to allow him the single.

Thus was the first half of the equation accomplished, persuading more than 10,000 optimists to throng the MCG that final morning. Nudge by nudge, nurdle by nurdle, the grail inched closer. Suddenly it was no more than a boundary away, but Botham and Miller dashed it from Border's lips. The game's very first replay screen was making its bow: it sure had a tale to tell its progeny.

Key moment: Miller's catch.
Sound bite: "He got out to the only shot he played. The rest he'd been blocking or leaving." (Greg Chappell on Thommo)

SYDNEY 1987

Means: Under duvet with Walkman and ex-girlfriend.
Scores: Australia 343 (Jones 184*, Small 5-75) and 251 (S Waugh 73,
Emburey 7-78); England 275 (Gower 72, Taylor 6-78) and 264
(Gatting 96, Sleep 5-72). AUSTRALIA won by 55 runs.
Material impact: None.

AT THE fag-end of a series of unremitting home gloom, something
to cheer, and lustily. Dean Jones's dominance, Steve Waugh's cool
resolve, Merv Hughes's bombast, Border's astute leadership, Peter
Sleep's ungainly but incisive leggies and, best of all, a star turn from
a chap known as "Peter Who?" England had regained the urn but
a fresh era had dawned.

Without "Deano" Australia would have been up shit creek and
paddle-free. He was still bedding down on the first morning when
allegedly reprieved: the fielders swore he'd nicked Gladstone Small,
prompting Mike Gatting's suggestion to umpire Steve Randell at
lunch: "Try some carrots". Unfazed, nimble feet and measured
aggression enabled him to make light of a surface already aiding
spin as well as seam: all told, he accounted for nearly 60 per cent
of the runs acquired during his nine-hour sojourn.

As Jones coaxed 111 runs out of the last three wickets there were
84 minutes of defiance from Peter Taylor, the offie from New South
Wales purportedly called up erroneously, in place of another Taylor,
M A. Another bit of low Aussie cunning? The reedy Taylor
proceeded to enmesh the England middle-order, his first three
trophies Lamb, Gower and Botham. Now the tide turned anew.
Emburey, Richards and Small kept the lead within bounds, Emburey
worked his way through the Australian top-order, and at 145 for
seven on the fourth day there was only one team tucking into its
lunch with any vigour.

Our friend Taylor wasn't done yet, however, and a 98-run stand
with Waugh set up a forbidding target of 320. At 91-1 and 233-
5 England were in front of the eight-ball, but after tea Border
turned to Waugh who soon duped Gatting into a return catch; Sleep
whipped through the rest, bowling Emburey with seven balls
remaining. Not since O'Reilly and Grimmett had England been

beaten by a pair of Aussie twirlers. A new age really was beckoning.

Key moment: Waugh's slower ball disposes of Gatting.
Sound bite: "I couldn't bear to watch the last few overs." (Gatting)

SYDNEY 1991
Means: Under duvet with Walkman and wife (not ex-girlfriend)
Scores: Australia 518 (Matthews 128, Boon 97, Border 78, Malcolm 4-128) and 205 (Healy 69, Tufnell 5-61); England 469-8 dec (Gower 123, Atherton 105, Stewart 91) and 113-4 (Gooch 54). DRAWN
Material impact: None.

THOSE DODGY DOMINOES of Brisbane and Melbourne were still tottering, the Biggles escapade impending: this brief illusion of competitiveness would have to suffice.

Bar Gower's sparkling effort the initial innings were leisurely and thrill-free, just as Australia would have wished: two-up after two Tests, they had merely to avoid defeat to retain the urn. Not till the fourth morning, indeed, did Gower and Stewart dispel the threat of the follow-on. If Graham Gooch had little option but to declare, it was an admirable gesture just the same. Phil Tufnell, duly hopped, skipped and jumped through the defences of Border, Boon and Jones as Australia, 38 for two entering the last day, staggered to 166 for seven. Had Gower not spilled Waugh at bat-pad, the Middlesex rapscallion would have gleaned an imperishable hat-trick.

Ian Healy was still there, still minding the watch, maiden Ashes fifty to his as-yet unsung name, but to English eyes the sight of Carl Rackemann was in no way perturbing. An injury-plagued quickie from Wongai, he came in trailing only slightly more pretensions to authentic batsmanship than a platypus. In the event he outlived Healy. After 72 minutes and 75 balls he broke his duck, the most dilatory start by any Australian. Fearful that one expensive over would prove too dear, Gooch declined to bring back Devon Malcolm until the blond Queenslander had hung around for the best part of two hours; with his sixth ball the Derbyshire man did the trick, though not before the match had been condemned to a quiet funeral.

Or so we thought. Needing a fanciful 255 in 28 overs, Gooch strode out with Gower and 84 runs cascaded from the first 12. "We put the wind up them," Gooch would brag. "It was great fun." It couldn't last, but it was hellish fun dreaming.

Key moment: Rackemann's first dot ball.
Sound bite: "There's more to playing Test cricket than just bowling."
(Gooch on Tufnell)

TRENT BRIDGE 1993

Means: Press box TV at Lord's and Maidstone; stepfather's ginormous Bang & Olufsen in Bournemouth.
Scores: England 321 (Smith 86, Hussain 71, Hughes 5-92) and 422-6 dec (Gooch 120, Thorpe 114*); Australia 373 (Boon 101, M Waugh 70, McCague 4-121) and 202-6 (Julian 56*). DRAWN
Material impact: None.

BORDER AND CO had strolled home in the first two Tests; desperation was biting hard. Not only did the home selectors plump for an XI numbering five fellows without Ashes experience – one of whom, Mark Lathwell, candidly admitted he wasn't yet worthy – they even stooped to drafting in an Irishman who'd taken the new ball for Western Australia. The first known instance, attested one visiting journo, of a rat joining a sinking ship. As it transpired, Martin McCague ignored the jibes and played a sizeable part.

For all Robin Smith's belligerence against Hughes and a cock-a-hoop Shane Warne, Nasser Hussain alone evinced any staying power on day one, grinding out 71 in four hours as England's last four wickets posted 101. David Boon's second consecutive century and Mark Waugh's elan notwithstanding, Australia were still 10 behind when their eighth wicket went, the stutter triggered by McCague and Mark Ilott, the Poms' greenest opening attack for 31 years.

Warne now swung productively, then bamboozled Lathwell and Smith as England limped to 122 for four by stumps on day three. Nightwatchman Andy Caddick clung on for a further hour but when Brendon Julian at last unglued him the lead was 107: far too skimpy for such an innocuous track. The implacable Gooch now found a resolute apprentice in Graham Thorpe, the Surrey southpaw becoming the 14th Englishman to mark his Test debut with a hundred. On the final morning Gooch opted to bat on for 40 minutes: conservative perhaps, but after seven defeats on the trot who could begrudge him a bit of a bask?

Hindsight being the harshest of mistresses, it may well have been England's undoing. Harried by Caddick, seduced by Peter Such, Australia lost five men between lunch and tea: the wobble was on. As it panned out, Steve Waugh did what Steve Waugh does best while Julian dispensed with inhibition, muscling to his half-century with a six and a grin. In a match celebrating youth, the only thing missing was a wink.

Key moment(s): Waugh at peace: 62 minutes without a run.
Sound bite: "Gooch should have declared earlier." (Illingworth of the *Express*)

THE OVAL 1997
Means: First day in flesh; *Sunday Times* sports desk.
Scores: England 180 (McGrath 7-76) and 163 (Thorpe 62, Kasprowicz 7-36); Australia 220 (Blewett 47, Tufnell 7-66) and 104 (Caddick 5-42, Tufnell 4-27). ENGLAND won by 19 runs.
Material impact: None.

BARELY eight sessions yet enough twists to keep a pretzel producer in profit for a decade or two. Final tally: 667 runs, 235.1 overs, three seven-fers, one 50 and a wicket every 25 minutes. In mind if not in body, the Aussies were already homebound, mission comfortably accomplished, but this was still more fun than a chimps' tea party – and every bit as messy. *Match of the Day* even had the decency to overlook Dennis Bergkamp and acclaim the victorious captain as its Chap of the Day.

Key moment: Caddick's juggling return catch to see off Healy.
Sound bite: "Spineless! Gutless! Useless!" (The *Mirror* after Day 1) ◗

DAVID GOWER
OLD TRAFFORD, AUGUST 1989

ALLAN BORDER
THE SAME DAY — AUSTRALIA HAD JUST REGAINED THE ASHES

Matthew Engel

My First Dig

Matthew Engel comes from
Northamptonshire and lives
in Herefordshire; he thinks
neither will win the County
Championship in his lifetime.
He was formerly cricket
correspondent of *The Guardian*.
He now writes for the paper on
a ridiculous range of subjects,
mostly non-sporting, and edits
Wisden Cricketers' Almanack. He
lists his recreation as "whingeing".

Favourite Ashes innings
David Gower's 72 at Perth in
1982-83, on the first day's Test
cricket I ever saw in Australia. It
was an exquisite, flawless diamond,
ended only by a fantastic catch.

**Australia win more often
because...** in the words of
the philosopher David Stove:
"Whereas Australians hate the
Poms, the Poms only despise the
Australians."

You have to understand the significance of the winter of 1962-63. The snow fell, as I recall, on Boxing Day. It stayed on the ground until March. In that time, over most of Britain, the temperature barely rose above freezing point.

In those days, the electricity system was more temperamental than it is now, and there were a good many power cuts. Sports like football and horse racing were effectively abandoned for the duration. At my school, we just ran cross-countries twice a week for an entire term. The previous winter had been cold too, and we were in a run of poor summers. The talk was not of global warming but of a new Ice Age. If, that is, the Russians and Americans didn't blow us to all to smithereens first. I seem to have had a pessimistic sort of childhood.

Some people still talk of the winter of 1946-47 as worse. I don't think it was as cold for as long, though there may have been more snow, and there was certainly less fuel and less food. But I was four years short of being born then, and the wartime generation were inured to tough times in a way we post-baby boomers never were.

And there was, in 1963, one distraction. In the mornings, our new transistor radios, which freed us from reliance on the National Grid, would pick up the commentaries from Australia of the Ashes series. I don't think the broadcasts were crackly, though they were staccato, and I'm sure Dansette never provided a tone control.

Australian commentators never had (and mostly still haven't) the easy, languid, poetic approach that we all loved so much from John Arlott, that drew us to Test Match Special "because he didn't just talk about the cricket". To them, this was deadly serious business. Their tone was sharp, crisp, and statistical: they gave the score after just about every ball of the eight-ball overs. Occasionally, they would mention the weather: it was always hot and sunny.

At boarding school I would listen, snuggling under my tartan travel rug, before the 7am wake-up call. In memory (and this is probably very English) England were always in trouble, usually because they had dropped catches. In the March 1963 *Playfair Cricket Monthly* (I have remembered this ever since, and I have found the page to prove it) there was a cartoon drawn by Royman Browne of a man swaddled in a dressing gown standing in an obviously freezing and candle-lit kitchen. Water is leaking from the ceiling down the back of his neck. A voice from the radio is saying: "Harvey – who was dropped three times before he was thirty – is now..." and the caption says: "Sometimes I say to myself – 'George, old man' – I say – 'why were you ever born?'"

In fact, England drew that series and could easily have won it. The Australians were never strong throughout the Sixties, and it was absurd, and unlucky, that in five series England never once managed to get the Ashes. But the Aussies seemed like a race of supermen, not from the far side of the planet, but from another planet entirely.

Even then, I knew I was never going to open the batting for England in a Sydney Test match. That wasn't really the point. I didn't just want to go to Australia. I wanted to BE an Australian: I wanted to have a no-nonsense, modern-sounding name, like Keith or Paul or Neil (no one except me was at that stage called Matthew); I wanted to be unstuffy and call everyone "mate". I'd still support England at cricket of course, but that was different.

A new boy came to school called Alex Bernstein. I asked where he came from and he said, with what must have been a mind-your-own-business sneer, "Western Australia". I bombarded him with questions about the place for six months before he eventually told me it was a joke and that he really came from Dublin, which was exotic enough when you're in the Thames Valley. I got over wanting to be called Keith. Eventually. The rest of it I never got over.

IT TOOK 20 YEARS. It might have been only 16. I was working at Reuters news agency, my first Fleet Street job, and was the obvious candidate to report the 1978-79 tour of Australia (well, I thought I was the obvious candidate, anyway) until they remembered that they had an experienced cricket reporter, Brian Williams, already working in the Sydney office. That was the end of that.

Within a year, I had joined *The Guardian*. It would be good to believe this was a reward for my obvious journalistic talent. In fact, they thought I was someone else entirely. I was offered a substantial pay cut and told I was expected to be a professional sub-editor and should forget any fancy-pants idea of going off anywhere to do any writing.

But this time my timing was right. John Arlott (not merely a hero now but a colleague – I was too overawed to look at him, never mind speak) was edging close to retirement. His presumed successor, Henry Blofeld, had had a blazing row with the paper and gone off to pursue a highly successful freelance career instead. The next in line was Paul Fitzpatrick, who was a classic old-fashioned *Manchester Guardian* man: nice, northern, gifted, unpretentious and deeply-rooted. Too deeply rooted, he decided soon enough, to spend his winters swanning round the world when there was rugby league to watch.

I found myself in the Dennis Price role in *Kind Hearts and Coronets*. Without actually bumping anyone else off (though some of the other sports sub-editors may have had their suspicions), a most improbable succession was taking place.

Sub-editing *The Guardian* in those days was not an especially creative job. We were expected to cut down the over-enthusiasm of the correspondents on those sports which didn't interest us much, like hockey and sailing, and leave everything else more or less alone. Changing the correspondents' copy was not encouraged. Most of the lads (all lads, then) were waiting for the great David Lacey to give over so they would get the chance to write about football. Twenty years on, some of them are still waiting. None of them cared about cricket. I was young, keen, not in love and (so one of the other subs told me in the Gunmaker's Arms one night) fairly ruthless in pursuing my own interests.

I flew to Australia in September 1982. I remember debating with myself whether or not I ought to pack a pullover, eventually deciding that there might be the odd cool evening somewhere and that I might as well. I was 31 years old.

When the ambition of a lifetime is fulfilled, when a boy's dream comes true, something has gone from one's life. I can never again cross the seas to Australia for the first time, never again tread for the first time an Australian cricket field and say: "Here it is – here's the place I've dreamed on..."
Neville Cardus, 1937

I still remember the feeling of anticipation I had when I first walked up the steps to the entrance of one of the great Australian cricket grounds. I showed my identification to one of those little men with big forearms who usually seem to hold positions of minor authority in Australia. "Vujjastree," he said sharply.

This was difficult. Quite a lot of Serbo-Croat is spoken in Australian cities, but one didn't really expect it at the entrance to the Gabba cricket ground in Brisbane. It took quite a while to sort out that he was ordering me round to the Vulture Street entrance. "Vulture Street? Which way's that, please?" "You know where it is," he snarled.

He was probably in an especially foul mood. This was no cricket match. We were in the middle of the Brisbane Commonwealth Games. For me, it was a curious piece of timing. These ended three days before the arrival of the England cricketers. *The Guardian*, alert to the chance of a saved air fare, asked me to cover the Games before the tour began. So the Gabba was being used for a demonstration of Australian Rules football.

Having grown up in a country where one untoward step on a cricket square can earn you a massive earful from an outraged groundsman, it was impossible to imagine that men could really be allowed to play football across the pitch two months before the start of an Ashes Test. But it was happening. No one except me thought it was unusual.

The Commonwealth Games is a curious event. The scale of it is

I wanted to **be** an Australian: I wanted a **no-nonsense** name like Keith or Neil almost Olympian, one of the last reminders of how much of the world was once coloured pink. Over the rest of the world, it means nothing at all. And it doesn't generate all that much enthusiasm in England, especially when it is being held in a remote place with a very different time-zone. The English generally assume that an event in which their country can win about 150 medals may not be worth all that much.

The Australians think differently: they love it. (The unchanging nature of this was glimpsed in 1998, when England refused even to send a team to the first-ever Commonwealth Games cricket tournament, but the Aussies became consumed by the idea of winning gold.) The 1982 Games were held in their country, and in their brashest, newest, and least self-critical city at that.

The lasting motif of the Games was the sound of a local TV commentator, Norman May, screaming over some long-forgotten swimming race: "IT'S GOLD, GOLD, GOLD FOR AUSTRALIA." He hardly ever mentioned who they beat. The *Daily Mail* called him one-eyed, which was unfortunate, since he really did only have one eye.

I found it all a little difficult to take. In the three days' free time before the cricketers arrived, I went up the coast with a couple of mates. It rained solidly. I wasn't sure I liked Australia.

WHEN NEVILLE CARDUS went on tour for *The Guardian* (then the *Manchester Guardian*) in 1936-37, the idea of journalists travelling with international cricket teams was in its infancy. Only a tiny press corps had gone from England to report the Bodyline tour four years earlier. And the Authorised Version now relates that all of them were either too nice (Jack Hobbs), too callow or too ignorant to tell readers back home exactly what England were doing that was so unpleasant.

Many more went with Cardus to see the series which England led 2-0 then lost, with Bradman once and for all establishing his mastery over Hammond. After the war, when newsprint was rationed and travel difficult, it took a while for the idea to take hold again. In the Fifties large numbers of journalists packed their dinner jackets, set sail from Tilbury and spent a month on board ship, playing bridge and deck quoits, gasping for air through the Gulf of Aden, then glimpsing Fremantle with an air of wonderment not much different from that experienced by Captain Cook.

In the Nineties English players, journalists and spectators on package tours turn up at cricket grounds anywhere on the planet with the casual air they would employ if travelling by Northern Line to The Oval. The ferocious class distinctions of the luxury liners have been reduced to the temporary differences between business class and economy. The journeys are flavourless. Ditto the food. No one dines at the captain's table.

In the early Eighties the magic of touring had not entirely disappeared. It still felt like an adventure. You had to be fairly determined still to cross the world for a two-week holiday, and the entire middle-class population of London did not descend on Sydney at New Year. These days the media corps – including TV camera-men, fixers, photographers, Internet reporters, freelances and chancers – can easily top 50. It is perfectly possible, with the help of the tour press officer, for a journalist to provide perfectly acceptable reports for an English newspaper without having to talk to a cricketer. Since the cricketers are increasingly suspicious of the press, and try wherever possible to stay in different hotels, and since conversations with most of them tend to be increasingly stereotyped and dull, this can suit everyone concerned.

In 1982 we were somewhere between these two worlds. No-one packed a dinner jacket. Players and press entertained mutual suspicion on an institutionalised level, but were amiable enough in the bar. It was difficult to avoid Ian Botham anywhere, never mind for four months. The schedule was modern-hectic; the mood still a little bit ancient-relaxed.

Cardus would have been obliged to send copy by telegram, every word charged for, which had an inhibiting effect on even the most lyrical adjectivalist. By the end of the Eighties, there were fax machines and modems, and newspaper offices thought nothing of ringing their reporters across the world several times daily. In 1982 this was still rather unusual. We communicated by telex, which involved typing out a report at the close of play, taking a walk, a taxi or (in Melbourne) a tram to a Government office, and handing the typescript to an operator.

For a newspaperman, the time difference between one country and another does not just mean jet lag; it affects the whole rhythm of your life. Most Australian cities are 11 hours ahead of London during the English winter. The great disadvantage of this is that by the time readers have a report of one day in front of them, they will already have heard via other means the next day's scores. This can make attitudinising and pontificating very risky indeed. The great advantage should be that there is plenty of time to write your report. It is even possible to read the following morning's Australian papers, realise you have made a terrible mistake and ring London to correct it before the first edition deadline.

This can turn into a disadvantage too. New to the job, anxious to impress my masters, uncertain of my ability and precious about my prose, I lost the fast and furious pace of newspaper writing, and began to spend hours at my desk, polishing. There was a precedent for this. Paul Fitzpatrick, my predecessor, would emerge from his room so late at night he became known as "Mole". By the time I had been to the telex, it was long past what Cardus (or a half-decent nutritionist) would have regarded as a sensible dinner-hour.

Then there was the paranoia. For a journalist, information is crucial. In the cloistered world of a cricket tour, the fear that everyone else knows something you don't can become overwhelming. At least it overwhelmed me. What if the representatives of every other English newspaper knew that Eddie Hemmings had a groin strain and would be unable to play in the next match? In one's head it can assume rather more importance than might be sensible to an objective observer. Once you know, you can place it in context and assess it sensibly. BUT WHAT IF YOU DON'T KNOW?

Sensible journalists paced themselves, sometimes ordered room service of an evening, stayed in to watch telly or read a book. Every time I tried that, two terrors set in: 1. The Hemmings groin-strain scenario; 2. The possibility that everyone else was having a great time and I wasn't. I was not paranoid enough to believe there was any conspiracy. If Eddie Hemmings did have a groin strain, my colleagues would tell me; Eddie might tell me himself. So even if there had been no cricket, and no late-night trip to the telex office, I would invariably wander down to the bar. The usual reprobates would be there, having the same conversations. And I would as usual drink far too much.

I GOT ILL – not ill-ill, but just debilitated. I began to look for bottles of Lucozade in corner shops as comfort. All my life I had envied people living in luxury air-conditioned hotel rooms. Now I discovered the rooms all looked the same, and that the air conditioning made you feel dreadful (eventually, I plucked up the courage to start turning the damn thing off, which is fine in those hotels which let you open the window). I began to long for beans on toast or a tomato sandwich. We were mostly staying in giant boxes in giant cities, moving between airports, telex offices and cricket grounds. Somewhere out there was Australia, but I wasn't part of it.

The cricket was wonderful, of course. England – their team weakened because several top players were banned for having gone to South Africa – were expected to lose the Ashes to an Australian team that had Lillee, Marsh and Greg Chappell back together again for the last hurrah. They did. But there was great excitement on the way.

In Perth, scene of a run-filled draw, David Gower played what I think was his greatest innings: a heavenly 72 ended by a near-impossible catch by John Dyson (still my favourite Ashes knock). England lost in Brisbane, where Kepler Wessels – doing his temporary impersonation of an Australian as a way round the ban on South Africa – scored a big hundred. They lost again in Adelaide where Bob Willis, eccentrically, chose to field first, then pulled back in Melbourne, thrillingly. They had an outside chance of holding on to the Ashes until midway through the Sydney Test. I enjoyed it all as a fan, wrote it down dutifully as a reporter. I kept reminding myself that I had achieved my life's ambition, and was being paid to do it.

Still, the little irritations kept taking over: in Brisbane, I hardly saw any cricket because the press box was so badly designed. All I saw was the large bald head and prominent ears of Dick Tucker, the correspondent of the *Sydney Sun*. We arrived in Adelaide with a storm blowing in off the Southern Ocean. I walked around in my summer jacket with the temperature down to about 50 Fahrenheit, and got ill yet again. Two days later it was closer to 50 Centigrade, and I felt terrible. In Melbourne, for the match against Victoria – always a depressing experience with the huge temple of the MCG empty and echoing – it got cold again, with the southerly blowing in from the Antarctic right into the press box. We lit the gas fires that were there to warm the Australian Rules reporters in a Melbourne winter. I envied Mike Carey, the *Daily Telegraph* correspondent, who had not merely brought a pullover but an anorak. We spent Christmas in the Melbourne Hilton, a hotel (as I wrote at the time) with "24-hour room service, though sometimes it takes a little longer". I was sociable, but never happy.

DUE TO A QUIRK of the itinerary the tour was more than halfway old before we set foot in Sydney. I seem to remember we were travelling by coach, presumably from the airport. We must have come out from an underpass and then glimpsed the Harbour Bridge and the Opera House in front of us. It was a perfect Australian summer's day. I think I may have cried.

As a traveller, I have grandly taken an attitude of proud scorn towards tourist cliches: I will always go to Chicago rather than Manhattan; the Grand Canyon never made as much impression on me as the Badlands of South Dakota; there are obscure palaces in India I would put ahead of the Taj Mahal; these days I am not absolutely sure Sydney is my favourite Australian city. But there was something about that moment quite unutterably magical. That evening, I went out to the Bridge and stared awestruck at the most wonderful cityscape I have ever seen. I even became obsessed with the rivets in the bridge. I was captivated. I could no longer care a stuff about Eddie Hemmings's groin. I was in Australia, dammit, and I was going to enjoy myself.

As in 1998-99, all the one-day games took place after the Test series. The cricket became unmemorable and more occasional. There were a lot of days off. I made friends in Melbourne and spent weekends at their beach house. I drove with Mike Carey from Adelaide to Sydney. I saw for the first time the Australian interior, how the landscape changes as you drive inland, to a deep red. In

Broken Hill, a huge dust-storm blew up and, in the morning light, as it cleared, we encountered our first kangaroo. I met a girl in Sydney, and we hit it off for long enough to release me from the frenzied late-night activity in the Bourbon & Beefsteak bar. I loved Australia. I have loved it ever since.

Since then, I have been back half-a-dozen times. In the late Eighties, I talked to the *Sydney Morning Herald* about taking a job there (as Cardus did). But I think I prefer Australia as a sort of mistress rather than a wife. I'm not sure I could live anywhere other than England. But there are still things in Australia that make me react the way I never would back home: there is a mumsy-song called "I Still Call Australia Home" that affects me the way no British equivalent ever could; I have been known to cry at the sight of gum-leaves against a deep blue Australian sky.

These days, I tour half-heartedly. Neither my work nor my family life lend themselves to long trips overseas. I'm still able to pop in to write about the odd Test match. The other correspondents resent me as a dilletante; I think I'm getting the best of every world. Sometimes, on my two very long tours of Australia, I would feel nostalgic for a roaring autumnal wind or a crisp, cold English winter's day. But never for a winter where the snow stayed from Boxing Day until March. ☽

DAVID BOON OLD TRAFFORD, AUGUST 1989

MIKE GATTING ADELAIDE, JANUARY 1995

Martin Johnson
Sneers and Loathing in Bendigo

Martin Johnson was the long-suffering cricket correspondent of *The Independent* through four consecutive Ashes hammerings, but thrice blessed in covering Mike Gatting's triumph in 1986-87. Foolish boy, on his first trip, thought all Ashes series would be like this. Finally could take no more, and defected to the *Daily Telegraph* as sports feature writer from 1996.

Favourite Ashes innings
Les Taylor's protracted duck in first Test innings, listened to on car radio. Brian Johnston's hysterics nearly had me off the road and into a ditch.

Australian cricketers are so manifestly superior because... we feel sorry for Australians living miles from anywhere, and like to give them something important to celebrate from time to time. Oh yes, and also because talent (of which we have plenty) is no good without the bottle to go with it.

Now that English children, weaned on a

24-hour diet of soap operas featuring semi-clad pubescent girls and acne-ridden peroxide youths, all speak with Australian accents, it is becoming increasingly difficult to tell the two nationalities apart. Two hundred years ago, the crewcut and the ball and chain around the leg was a bit of a giveaway, but sadly, this eminently sensible way of keeping our colonial cousins in order has been phased out by sentimental, left-wing do-gooders.

Nowadays, the simplest way, perhaps, is to attend a cricket match, in which one team will declare at 720 for 2, and the other one will be all out for 12. However, given that England and Australia are not always playing each other at cricket, and for the sake of our sanity we give thanks for that, some other clear distinction needs to be identified – and the answer, is, of course, that you can always tell an Australian by his subtlety.

It was a character trait that first sprang to international prominence when the Australian Prime Minister Paul Keating put his hand upon the Queen's person, and while many people wailed that this was a breach of protocol of seismic proportions, it seemed to me that the PM's act of putting his hand around Her Majesty's waist – instead of following the true Australian inclination on putting it on her bottom – indicated the very highest form of statesmanship. In similar circumstances, you could never have relied upon Sir Alec Douglas Home, or Ted Heath, to get it right.

The New Ball

This unique Australian characteristic first came home to me on my first visit there for an Ashes series, the last one that England won. It is too long ago for most people to remember, but suffice to say that Graham Gooch and Methuselah were opening the batting for the Old Testament XI versus the Phillistines.

There I was walking up Brisbane High Street, and approaching me on a gloriously hot afternoon was a lady of around 60 years of age, walking one of those ridiculous-looking poodles that have just been in for the full blow-dry and manicure. However, what caught my eye rather more was the front of her T-shirt, which said, simply, "Pommy". Not surprisingly, I glanced backwards as we passed, and there upon the back was the completion of the message: "Bastards".

I HAVE SINCE come to realise that when an Australian says, "G'day yer Pommy bastard", it is actually a term of endearment. So it should be. After all, it was us Poms who first introduced them to round-the-world cruises (single ticket only), including free weevil biscuits, first-class accommodation in the basement, and finally, breathtaking views of Botany Bay. The fact that many of them complained to the tour operators – in the same way as those whingeing Brits who used to travel to Spain and expect their hotel to be fully built – was just an early example of their lifelong ingratitude to the mother country.

Actually, in cricketing terms, Australians are far more subtle than the old Pommy Bastard T-shirt, as I discovered upon entering the gents at the Woolloongabba ground in Brisbane shortly after the first Test had ended in victory for England. Just above the toilet roll was an arrow, and written alongside the arrow was: "Australian batsman's application form".

The best example of subtle humour, however, came several years later, during a period in which beating England at Test cricket had almost become too routine to get excited about any more. It was at the WACA, in Perth, I think, when the usual influx of British tourists had resulted in banners draped all around the ground, bearing such witty messages as "Bristol Rovers Rule Okay" and "Hello Mum".

However, on the popular side of the ground licensed to sell beer (all Australian grounds have "dry areas", where it is safe to take the wife and kids, and no-one throws up before lunchtime), there was a giant banner which read: "Hide The Ashes Under A Bar of Soap". This, of course, being a reference to the popular Australian myth that personal hygiene and your average Pom do not often come together. Ergo, nothing so dry as a Pommy's towel, etc, etc, yawn, yawn.

The belief among Australian cricket watchers that Pommies do not take a shower may have something to do with the fact that, in recent years anyway, no English batsman has been at the crease long enough to require one. However, it is simply not true that an Englishman's reaction to a shower cubicle is much the same as Dracula's upon being asked if he would like to start with the garlic prawns in a Transylvanian bistro, any more than it is true that all Australian males old enough to shave (which eliminates all their soap actors) wear corked hats and sport enormous beer bellies. Well, they don't all wear corked hats anyway.

The first and only time I recall seeing an Australian wearing a corked hat was in Bendigo, where England were not only paying a visit, but, if memory serves, also failing to lose for once to some local team cobbled together with old lags and young bucks. He was sitting – although I use the term loosely as his head was firmly resting on the beer pump – at a bar stool, and appeared to be entirely comatose.

Not that this excited much attention, nor did it when he suddenly woke up, and was violently ill in the well beneath him normally reserved for cigarette butts. This, of course, only made him thirsty again, and a couple of thumps on the bar was all the information the serving wench required to recognise his need for replenishment. Glass duly filled, he downed it one, was immediately sick again, and went back to sleep. This, presumably, passes for normal behaviour in Bendigo, as no-one turned a hair.

The only other occasion that I have been personally spellbound by an Australian's performance at the bar was in a Sydney night club, packed so tight that you couldn't have got a fag paper between those occupying the stools. For one particular chap this was good news, as he was incapable of personal support, and was only kept upright as he reached out in a vain attempt to locate his drink by his next door neighbour. And when the neighbour left her stool to go to the ladies,

The New Ball

I watched in fascination for his next attempt to find his pint. This time, deprived of the necessary safety net, he continued his journey sideways, cracked his head on the floor, and began bleeding rather copiously. An ambulance was summoned, of course. Ha! Do me a favour. He was removed to a dark corner of the bar – where his bleeding was in less danger of staining anyone's shirt – propped up against the wall, and abandoned. He never, at any stage, appeared to feel a thing.

ONE OF THE FIRST THINGS I discovered about Australians is that they are totally paranoid about being roughly four million miles from anywhere else. As a consequence, they have this burning desire to travel, which is why you will not find yourself served with a pint of beer anywhere in London, or even the Home Counties, by an accent that is not considerably closer to Sydney than Sidcup.

And for those who don't travel, the thirst for knowledge from the outside world is unquenchable. Ergo, when you are identified as a Pom, you are immediately pumped for information about anything to do with England, as though you were a dark green tellytubby who had just landed in an alien craft.

On my first Ashes trip for *The Independent*, I was warned by one of the older journalists to be a bit careful what I wrote, as the Aussies were forever running what were known as "quotebacks". This, given their desperate need to find out what the rest of the world was saying and thinking, was a vehicle for regurgitating chunks of English newspaper comment to their readers. You would never pick up the *Daily Mirror* in England and see an entire page devoted to what Bill Bloggs of the Wagga Wagga Bugle was saying about the Test match, but in Australia, it's big stuff.

Sadly, I forgot the lesson, and after three matches on tour, during which England had hovered between hopeless and unmentionable, I decided that a spot of good news ought to be relaid to those readers getting a little anxious about England's Test match prospects. "Fear not," I wrote, or something like it, "there are only three things wrong with England at the moment. They can't bat, they can't bowl, and they can't field."

Next morning, the Australian papers arrived, and the front page

Australia reveal themselves to be crap and can you find the Test score? Can you heck

of one of them was entirely taken up with, in huge type, "CAN'T BAT, CAN'T BOWL, CAN'T FIELD!"

Underneath, it said: "Latest on pathetic poms, see page 13". And there, on page 13, was near as dammit a full page of quotes from what we pathetic hacks had been penning on our lousy cricket team. So what happens? England win the first Test, and the cricketers all start walking about in "Can't Bat" etc T-shirts.

The fact that Australia went on to lose a series they were unbackable favourites to win before the start sent the nation into a total decline. Beforehand, people like Craig McDermott and Merv Hughes were regularly wheeled onto chat shows, and even the weatherman, a complete crackpot wearing a bow-tie, spent most of his morning cracking feeble jokes about English cricket. "Wet and windy down in Melbourne today, and that's just inside the Pommy dressing room." That kind of thing.

The Australians like winning, you see, and this perception of their remoteness also makes it headline news whenever they win something internationally, no matter how obscure or remote. Hence, some farm labourer from Alice Springs wins a minor tiddlywink tournament in Kuala Lumpur, and it leads the six o'clock news. Unless, that is, some visiting diginatary is visiting the PM in Canberra, such as the Polynesian Minister for Prophylactics. Anyone visiting Australia, and thus underlining its huge importance in the global nature of things, gets first item on the news, and it's just hard luck on you if you're from Woollongong and have finished second in the Tokyo International Egg and Spoon race. Tough on yer mate, as they say. You're relegated to second item on the six o'clock bulletin.

However, if Australians are second to none (apart from the Americans of course) at trumpeting their successes, then they are world champions also at ignoring their failures. When the 1986-87 Ashes series began, they could not get enough of the Pathetic Pom angle. Botham's a has-been, Gower's a prima donna, Gatting's too fat, Dilley can't bowl a hoop downhill. Everywhere you went, there were pictures of Allan Border beaming out of the newspapers, and Bill Lawry on the telly shaking his head sadly at England's prospects.

Then, bingo. Australia reveal themselves to be utterly crap, and can you find the Test score? Can you heck. Take hold of a magnifying glass, and look closely at that six-point type just below the greyhound results. Yes, there it is! England 450-4 declared, Australia 73-6. By the time England were actually clinching the Ashes in Melbourne at Christmas, the giant video screen at the MCG had totally given up showing the cricket replays. Instead, we got Pat Cash, the Australian, playing tennis in the Davis Cup. Needless to say, he was winning.

HOWEVER, what bugs some people most about the Australians is their slavish devotion to all things American. We are far from blameless ourselves (count up how many people tell you to have a nice day the next time you're out shopping) and I have to say also that British Airways have cottoned on to this ghastly American expression (amazing how they invent words) to "deplane". Americans also never say "now". They say "at this time". Ergo, when they want you to get off one of their aeroplanes, they say: "Ladies and gentleman, at this time it is our pleasure to deplane you." Ye gods.

However, back to the Australian obsession with Americana, beginning with the old trick of staging a sporting contest between two teams and calling it a World Series. This is marginally better than the American trick, which involves calling a game between only American teams a "World Series" but even this backfired on Australia when they fielded a first team and a second team in a World Series knockout tournament involving England. England were so hopeless, that Australia ended up with a best-of-three final between their first and second XIs, and were calling it a World Series.

Something else they have got from the Americans is the decision to treat all sporting crowds as morons unless specifically proved otherwise. It is now totally impossible to attend an international cricket match in Australia without being "entertained". And by this, I mean having your eardrums continually assaulted by some pillock on the tannoy, and being quite unable to start a match without the ball being delivered by parachute. Then, at lunchtime, they have dogs jumping through hoops, or balancing frisbees on their noses, all taking place to the loudest musical accompaniment imaginable.

Then there is the urge for hype and gimmicry, which in 1992

The New Ball

made the Australian Cricket World Cup publicity machine far more awesome than the cricket team. In fact, the only trick they missed was failing to paint the words "Benson and Hedges" on the roof of Sydney Opera House. The worst thing of all, however, was the official World Cup song, entitled "Who'll Rule The World", a classic of its kind, and released, would you believe, on the Sloggett label.

The lyrics were something else.

You're on the edge of your seat, feelings running high,
They're the best in the world, they make that white ball fly.
It's the dream of every man, to play the best that he can,
It's the fire deep inside, that keeps this game alive.
Who'll rule the world? Who'll Rule the World?
Gotta see who'll rule the world...

Etc, ad nauseam, aaaaargh.

The other abiding memory of that World Cup was the Australian-designed playing regulations in the event of rain, clearly devised by someone inside an institution dribbling down a bib and restricted to eating meals with plastic cutlery. In the England-South Africa semi-final, South Africa required 22 runs from 13 balls and a breathtaking finish was on the cards. Then it rained. They came back out again at 10.03pm, and despite the official finishing time of 10.15, South Africa's target had been revised to 21 runs to win from, er, wait for it, one delivery. This, to no-one's huge surprise, proved just beyond them.

The Australian marketing department is perhaps at its most fearsome before a Test series, perhaps mindful of the fact that Test cricket appears to be too subtle nowadays for Australian spectators, unable to cope with the concept of white clothing, red balls, and batsmen occasionally not attempting to belt the thing into Sydney High Street. You can imagine an old timer taking his grandkids to a Test match in Australia.

"What's that strange group of people standing over there grandad?" "That, lads, is what we call three slips and a gully."

However, Australia would never market a Test series on the grounds that it is occasionally more subtle than its bastard offspring.

When England were there not so long ago, the trailer opened to a montage of soaring sixes and exploding stumps, all to the backcloth of frantic music. And, just in case anyone was in any doubt as to the identity of the opposition, the major star was Henry Blofeld, playing the archetypal Pom. Dressed in full Henley regatta regalia, straw boater, striped jacket, the works, Henry's script required him to say things like: "If you like your cricket tough, tight and tummy-twisting, this is for you."

Blowers was also cast as the pinstriped city gent, complete with bowler hat and monocle, leaning over a bar, sandwiched between an Aborigine and a bloke – yes, you've guessed it – wearing a corked hat. This time, to the accompaniment of a doffed hat, Henry's line is: "You lot could do with a few bowlers."

FINALLY, any doctor asked to make an examination of Australia would diagnose an acute case of patriotism. This manifests itself in many different ways, including a breakfast cereal ad I once saw in which a little girl chirrups: "I love Australia, and I love my corn flakes." Implying, of course, that Rice Krispie addicts are liable to be strung up for high treason.

In England, of course, we take the opposite approach, and it is doubtful whether anyone in their right mind would use the Union Jack to try and sell anything. In victory, we are suspicious ("Ah yes, but they had one or two injuries...") while in defeat, we take refuge in black humour ("England lost again Fawlty." "Did it Major?") When England lose at anything, the so-called guilty men are lampooned as root vegetables by tabloid newspaper cartoonists, or else dressed up in dunce's caps. In fact, if and when England start winning at cricket on a regular basis, half the average pub conversation will be cut out at a stroke.

However, it would be a dull old world if we were all the same, and there would be no more calamitous effect on Australian pub conversation if us Brits suddenly stopped whingeing and started taking bathtime a bit more seriously. The fact of the matter is, Pommy bastards and bloody convicts are actually rather fond of each other. ◗

NASSER HUSSAIN OLD TRAFFORD, JULY 1997

GLENN MCGRATH LORD'S, JUNE 1997

Scyld Berry

The Most Durable Rubber

Scyld Berry has been cricket correspondent of *The Sunday Telegraph* since 1993. He began at *The Observer* in 1976, and has since covered more than 200 England Test matches. He has written five books, four of them on cricket, and lives near Bath with three children, two cats, one dog and a wife, playing club cricket when they allow.

Favourite Ashes innings
Has to be Ian Botham's 149 not out at Headingley in 1981, for creating hope where none was. The one I haven't seen has to be Jack Brown's 140 at Melbourne in 1895.

Australia have had their nose, legs and arms in front of late because... a lesser English system has produced lesser players, or at any rate no great ones, like several contemporary Australians. Usually, too, England have been too ill-prepared or stale to do their best.

Of the last five Ashes series, before this

winter, four have been far too one-sided to command the greatest
interest, let alone excitement. In 1990-91 and 1994-95 England were
stale when they arrived in Australia in October, having started the
calendar year in the West Indies and gone through a six-Test summer
as well. In 1989 and 1993 Allan Border's men, hectored by Merv
Hughes, trampled over all in their way and forced the resignations
of David Gower and Graham Gooch from the captaincy. In all four
of these series Australia were 2-0 up after two Tests, and the outcome
foregone, so bowed were England. Only in 1997, at long last, did
England make a series of it and fight sufficiently for the pendulum
to swing to and fro.

Ashes series, however, were not always one-sided, the younger
generation may be pleased to hear. In fact the Ashes took off as the
first major sporting contest between countries separated by the seas
as a result of a five-Test series that was anything but one-sided. After
four Tests of the 1894-95 series the score stood at two-all; and, no
less significantly, the other elements which have gone into making the
Ashes a topic of national interest in England and Australia, and the
rest of the cricket world, all came together in this series.

A hundred years on David Frith wrote a book about it, *The First
Great Test Series*. He wrote that Queen Victoria, "not renowned
for her interest in cricket, became curious as the excitement rose".
She did not sit in front of the satellite coverage all night with a supply

of cans, we may suppose, tearing her hair-net out when an England wicket fell, but she did demand to be kept abreast of the scores. So did the rest of the British, or at least English, sporting public. It was when Test cricket took off and rose to the position it holds today, or even higher.

PREVIOUS TOURS to Australia had been private commercial ventures which seldom came near to assembling the representative strength of English cricket. They were often ill-timed as well, coming one winter after another, or worse still, like 1887-88, when two such English teams toured Australia at the same time. But in 1894 the Melbourne Cricket Club and the trustees of the Sydney Cricket Ground combined as the nearest force to an overall authority before the foundation of the Australian Cricket Board. Moreover, all previous Ashes series except one had failed to hit upon the correct length: as everyone except some of today's administrators knows, one or two or three Tests are insufficient for the dramatic content to be maximised (while six are too many). So it was that five Tests were arranged, the dramatically right number, like the acts in a Shakespeare play.

Brisbane and Perth were just frontier towns, but Adelaide had already staged a Test match, and was offered another to make a change from Sydney and Melbourne, which staged two each. The Englishman contracted by the Melbourne and Sydney authorities was Andrew Stoddart. He had already gone on two tours of Australia and had captained England before in WG Grace's absence, and more importantly still, he came much cheaper than WG. The party of 12 other players whom Stoddart assembled was nearer to fully representative than any hitherto from England. A tour fee of £300 which could be safely banked – enough to buy a fine house in most parts of the country – attracted eight of the best professionals. WG himself did not join the party, but in 1894 he was widely assumed to be fading away, as he had every right to do at the age of 46, which only served to make his following annus even more mirabilis. Otherwise, only FS Jackson of the amateurs, who never toured, and Bobby Abel of the professionals, were notable omissions.

Stoddart, furthermore, selected wisely in terms of the characters of his men and nurtured a team spirit which carried his party through to the end. The England players of 1990-91, who were condemned to more and more naughty-boy nets the more they failed, did not pool together to buy their captain a silver tobacco jar. Mike Atherton, on the following tour, when lumbered by Ray Illingworth with too many old players, did not present each of them afterwards with a diamond scarf-pin.

England used only 12 players in the whole series of 1894-95, against Atherton's party a century later which comprised 22 cricketers in all at different times. Stoddart's 13th player was the Sussex lob bowler, Walter Humphreys, which suggests a pre-modern if not antediluvian game: but he was used in the up-country games, against XVIII of Bathurst or XXII of Ballarat, when it was necessary to rest England's two main bowlers. The Test series itself contained the elements we recognise as modern.

The Test grounds in Sydney and Melbourne had grown to accommodate crowds over 20,000 (the MCG had fitted in 35,000 for an Australian Rules game). They had nets where the players practised before each game under keen local eyes, for this was no longer a game played for fun alone, if it ever was in Australia. Before the opening Test in Sydney, the Australians did not practise on the immediately preceding day, but they did for two mornings before that, and some of the players in the afternoon as well. After these two morning sessions, too, the Australians had fielding practice, which suggests a seriousness of purpose which did not increase much, if at all, until the advent of fully professional cricket with Kerry Packer's World Series.

The Australian newspapers chronicled the 1894-95 series in great depth, listing almost every run, and where it was scored, and the fielder, so it is possible to make some sort of judgement on the fielding standards, without a ball being captured on film. I deduce that standards were fairly high, higher than we might have supposed, since the Australians were loudly condemned for their "wretched" fielding in the Sydney Test after dropping six – but only six – distinct chances. England, who only arrived from Toowoomba 36 hours before the start, dropped three.

To encourage fielders, and a high standard, the outfields other than Adelaide's were smooth, at any rate by comparison with the bumpy fields which had been the rule. Sydney's pitch had a surface of black soil brought in from the country. It was prepared not only by Ned Gregory, one of Australia's first great cricket clan and the resident groundsman at the SCG, but also by a two-ton roller pulled by a horse that wore special leather shoes. Scoreboards were as informative as any in England a century later, though not as comprehensive as they were to become in Australia: they gave the score of every batsman in the current innings but not his mode of dismissal. The over consisted of six balls by now in Australia (though not yet in England), which was again the ideal number, though a hit over the fence still counted for no more than five runs.

The balls were Duke's brought out from England: not until after the Second World War were Australian balls used for an Ashes series. Most of the bats used by the home players were imported from England too, at considerable cost: club bats made by Warsop's or Francis Dark or Ayres were being advertised in the papers at a sale price of around one pound. One of Australia's opening batsmen, William Bruce, a Melbourne lawyer and presumably prosperous, used a bat which had a chunk knocked out of it in mid-Test and replaced it with another one which had also "seen better days". It was an interesting development, therefore, when Syd Gregory, son of groundsman Ned, made his double-century in the opening Test with a bat made in Australia. Whether the willow came from England was not reported, but the cheers went up from the crowd as the president of the NSW Cricket Association said as much, before presenting Gregory with a collection of more than a hundred pounds.

Time-keeping was not punctual. In Melbourne the day's play tended to start about five minutes later than the appointed hour of midday, and about 10 minutes later in Sydney. Some – to us, quaint – conventions were still observed and retained the element of chivalry. When an England player was injured in the first Test, Charlie Turner of the Australian team acted as substitute at first, before England's 12th man took over. When Turner in turn arrived late for the start one morning, the favour was returned by an English substitute.

But if vestiges of high Christian principle lingered – and there was no suggestion that the "enemy" sub would do anything but his best – the seriousness with which the series was conducted cannot be questioned. Stoddart was reported to look shattered when he lost the toss in the final Test, and with it the chance to bat first, and to win, or so he thought. Disappointment was shown by William Brockwell when he dropped a slip catch; and by the Australian wicketkeeper Arthur "Affie" Jarvis when his appeal for a catch was turned down (Jarvis kept staring skywards as if for justice); and something like outright dissent was apparent when the England amateur Francis Ford was given out stumped in the first Test. According to the *Sydney Morning Herald*: "Blackham barely had the bails off before he dropped the ball, the batsman seeming rather doubtful as to the accuracy of the umpire's decision." A century before modern commentators denounced players for their chatter, the players on both sides were reported to have shouted "catch it" while the ball was in the air. Cordiality and fraternal feeling marked the relationship of the teams off the field, but on it the cricket was more than mere sport.

The popular interest aroused by the opening Test, and by the rest of the series until its climax, had no precedent in sport, and also transcended it. Frith quotes one Australian editorial: "It has been left to Mr Stoddart and his companions to take the Australian public by storm, and for at least four months to make cricket the question of the day. Politics local and Imperial, the war in the East, currency tangles and municipal corruption in the United States, diplomatic intriguing, with possibly grave complications resulting therefrom, have been cast into the shade. Nothing, in short, has been able to withstand the avalanche-like progress of the Stoddart combination." By the fifth Test in Melbourne, businesses there were said to have stuck up notices requesting that cricket should not be discussed on the premises, to what avail we cannot know.

As for Sydney, the *Sydney Morning Herald* reported that "huge crowds have stood patiently day after day in King-street and in Pitt and Hunter streets... Outside the *Herald* office the scores were posted throughout the day with great speed, intervals of but about two to three minutes intervening between the announcements, so that those gathered before the board were able to follow closely the fortunes of the game. Never before has Sydney been in such continuous rapid telegraphic communication with Melbourne. Two or three minutes sufficed to send a telegram through and within 10 minutes of the fall of a wicket at the Southern cricket ground (MCG) the news of the event was all over this metropolis." The mass of the people, in other words, were keen for something to entertain or distract them: some national enterprise which took them out of themselves. "Out of a game, cricket had evolved into a mighty struggle between the old world and the new."

By the 1891 census, 75 per cent of Australia's population was native-born: the people were rooting for Australia, yet retained some allegiance for the home of their parents. Australia after the gold-rushes was not so prosperous either; there was poverty enough for many to need some escape from daily reality. It was not long before this first great series, at the end of the 1880s, that Henry Lawson, just out of his teens, came to Sydney and wrote:

They lie, the men who tell us, for reasons of their own,
That want here is a stranger, and that misery's unknown;
For where the nearest suburb and the city proper meet
My window-sill is level with the faces in the street –
Drifting past, drifting past,
To the beat of weary feet –
While I sorrow for the owners of those faces in the street.

If the Australian public was gripped – the last Test was watched by crowds in excess of 100,000 – so too were the English. Again for the first time, reports of the Test matches reached England quickly and regularly enough to excite the appetite. The romance of such an adventure was enormous; distance does lend enchantment. England's cricketers, to all intents the national team, had gone away for over seven months, sailing for several weeks to the other side of the world via Port Said and Ceylon. No other international cricket, whether England-South Africa or United States-Canada, offered anything like the same well-matched skills. No wonder Queen Victoria wanted to know the score, especially after the first Test. *Wisden*'s comment that this was "probably the most sensational match ever played in either Australia or in England" may still not be out of date.

THE SEE-SAWING began when the Australians lost their first three wickets for 21 runs then recovered to make 586, the highest Test score to date (the word "Test" was now commonly used in the press, though the first "official" such match, when the home team was chosen by fully representative selectors for the first time, was still five years away). The Australians had gathered in their dressing room shortly before midday, and had elected Jack Blackham as their captain: this election process had started before the very first Test match in 1876-77, such was the democratic spirit in the "new" land.

Blackham tossed with Stoddart on the ground, and play began at 12.12 with Tom Richardson bowling three top-order Australians in his opening spell. It would be surprising, given the overall improvement in human athletic activity, if Richardson had anything like the 90 mph speed of the quickest moderns. Yet he was quick enough to dismiss Joe Darling first ball with a yorker, and for another ball to hit the batsman's pad and his stumps and still to roll on to the boundary; and to strike another batsman over the heart on the second day. When Australia's champion all-rounder George Giffen went in at number three, he kept looking at a "rise" or ridge in the middle of the pitch. When he had made 38, Giffen fended "a bumpy ball" off the handle of his bat to the keeper's left and to cries of "catch it". Otherwise, "his defence was perfect, and his off-hitting and drives were remarkably clean and hard", according to the *Sydney Morning Herald*, as he compiled 161. To that Syd Gregory added 201, spread over the first and second days but only four and a half hours in all. The attitude of the 24,000 crowd was illustrated when Gregory overtook Giffen's 161. "They rose as by common instinct and cheered again and again": if Giffen was the undisputed champion of Australia, Gregory was the champion of New South Wales.

All through the series England's attack was carried by Richardson and Bobby Peel, who both averaged around 60 overs per Test. Richardson took 32 wickets at 26 each; Peel, classified as a slow left-armer, was quicker than Johnny Briggs, their only assistant of note, and took the new ball, pushed it through and conceded little more than two runs per over. Their field settings were strange to our eyes, though they both specialized in what the Victorians called off-theory. Peel usually posted all nine of his fielders on the off side, and Richardson eight, even though his stock ball was the breakback, like an off-cutter produced by the swing of his shoulders. The convention was that it was caddish to hit an off-side ball to leg, but times were changing. Affie Jarvis, one of the Australian tailenders, played something which sounds like a sweep, while the big hitter Jack Lyons liked to pull. By the next tour Ranjitsinhji was leg-glancing balls that pitched on his stumps or even to the off-side, and the highest form of batsmanship pragmatically became what it is today, as leg-sided as off-sided.

England scored 325 in their first innings, and had to follow-on: not until 1900 did the side which held a large first-innings lead have any say in the matter. Two factors, however, came to England's aid when they followed on. One was that Blackham damaged his thumb in taking a ball from Lyons and had to be replaced behind the stumps by a couple of colleagues who, in turn, proved far less competent than the man recognised as the first modern wicketkeeper. The second was that rain fell but not, as yet, in a quantity which turned the pitch into glue. Rather, the damp and cloudy weather seemed to bind the pitch together during England's second innings and stop it crumbling. England knocked off the arrears and finally moved into credit. The number-consciousnes of the crowd was evident when England's most consistent batsman Albert Ward, who had made 75 in his first innings, surpassed it in his second: "a round of cheering" marked the feat. When Ward was on 28 second time round, he had edged a catch from the off-spin of Giffen, who had shouted "catch it", but the emergency wicketkeeper could not hold on.

By four o'clock on the fifth day, however, Australia wanted no more than 177 to win, and went for them. Lyons the opener blasted 25 out of 26 runs in the first quarter of an hour until he was bowled. Richardson was his usual wholehearted self, and only two runs could be added in the next quarter of an hour, but then Richardson was unwell and had to leave the field. England's fielding became slack as if resignation was setting in. By the close – it was the first Test to go into a sixth day – Australia were 113 for two. Even Queen Victoria

Stoddart had **captained** England before; more importantly, he came much **cheaper** than WG must have given up.

That evening dark clouds gathered, rain fell hard throughout the night, and in the morning the sun was hot. The legend that Peel, renownedly bibulous, needed a cold shower to sober up before the resumption – like every other Englishman, he had given up the game as lost – is too persistent to be ignored. The trouble was worth his while. Darling noticed that in Peel's first over a divot came out of the pitch which was half as big as his hand. At the other end Richardson was able to make the ball cut in nearly a foot and to make it lift. The batsmen couldn't get much of a foothold either, even though sawdust was brought out by the bucket for them and the bowlers. Between overs the batsmen patted the pitch down.

Yet the wickets did not fall at first. Darling smote a leg-side five off Peel. Giffen snicked a four off Richardson that sounded like a Chinese cut. The 61 runs which England had left to play with overnight were being whittled away. Then Darling went to hit Peel again, only to sky it to long-on, where Brockwell ran in, steadied himself and took the catch. Better still, the pitch was firming up under the hot sun so the bowlers could do even more on it, especially when Briggs replaced Richardson. Frank Iredale skied a return catch to Briggs. Joe Reedman and Gregory took the score to 158 – 19 to make, five wickets left – at which point Gregory went to cut Peel and was caught behind. "Even then," according to the *Sydney Morning Herald*, "people did not realise the danger."

At this juncture a freak of fortune favoured England and their none-too dexterous wicketkeeper Leslie Gay, who was replaced after this match. Reedman went out to Peel, missed, and the ball hit Gay on the chest before rebounding on to the stumps. Turner and Ernest Jones were both soon caught from attacking strokes. The injured Blackham and Charlie McLeod had 15 to make. They had not made enough when Blackham drove a return catch to Peel, and England had won by 10 runs. It was not until 1981 at Headingley that England or any other Test team next won a match after following on. The lunch which followed was a convivial affair for the touring side, whose health was proposed by the NSWCA president Mr Sheridan. Mr Stoddart said in his reply that he had a team of triers, yet acknowledged that the Australians had been robbed of victory by the weather.

THE BEACON WAS LIT. Cricket was now perceived as a test of the cricketing strength and general merit of the two countries. And the two-sided nature of the remainder of the series made sure that the drama did not abate.

England were sent in after rain in the second Test at Melbourne, and won by 94 runs. They were dismissed for 75, limited Australia to 123, then made 475 on a pitch that was dry and rolled and mown after the rest day. So England were two-nil up after two Tests, like Australia so often were a century or so later, but this time the team that was behind bounced back.

The Adelaide Test was staged in great heat, and England wilted in front of the smaller crowds (the city was far smaller than Sydney and Melbourne which had populations of almost half a million). Local gossip had it that Peel was deep in his cups: circumstantial evidence is that he, a fine all-rounder at times, made consecutive pairs in the Tests England lost. A cartoon depicted the visitors in a pub, some of them under the table. Another source of gossip derived from the fact that half of them were unmarried – and that half were married (rumour has always had a field day when cricketers go on tour). Society ladies flocked to the matches: reports emphasise how well-dressed and well-behaved the crowds were, to keep up colonial appearances. Another possible source of tension was the class division between the eight professionals and five amateurs who stayed in separate hotels in the main cities. But together this English team held the line. When Peel needed a drink, of whatever kind, while batting during the final Test, it was the amateur Ford who took it out for him.

In the fourth Test at Sydney Stoddart became the first England captain to send a team in, and lost, his side dismissed twice on the third day for 65 and 72 (the two examples set in this series seem to have deterred emulators until the West Indian fast bowling era began in the late 1970s and teams were regularly sent in.) Played on a wet wicket, this match was finished in two days' playing time. Briggs and Charlie Turner became the first bowlers from their respective countries to reach 100 Test wickets.

Two matches apiece, and almost a month to go before the final Test. Time for most of the Empire to digest the news and anticipate the concluding contest, and for Australian cricket-lovers to travel to Melbourne if they weren't already there. Perhaps the suspense of waiting was a little drawn out, but better that than back-to-back Tests within a fortnight starting on Boxing Day.

But if there were a few signs of cracks in the English team, so too in the Australian. During the interim newspapers published the averages for the series to date, but not in the way that you would have expected. The Australian averages were printed in three sets: one for the NSW players, another for the Victorian players, a third for the South Australians. The political background was that the Commonwealth of Australia was not to be inaugurated until the first day of January 1901. As yet there were no states but colonies. Lord Hopetoun, who became the first Governor-General of Australia, was the Governor of Victoria at this time, and keenly attended the vital Test in Melbourne. Indeed, as the belief grew that the colonies should unite under an Australian flag, cricket was seen as a prophetic example by showing what could be achieved when Australians pulled together, instead of going their own way by, for instance, building different railway gauges in each colony. The players still had no national colours: they usually wore the cap of the host authority or club. But they personified the possibilities.

For the immediate moment, though, too many cricketers were selected to represent pre-Federation Australia. The last couple of marginal selections in each team seemed to go in favour of local players. Thus 22 in all were required by Australia, against England's 12, or 11 once Gay had been replaced for the last four Tests by Hylton Philipson. But one debutant was spectacularly successful, when the Victorian Albert Trott was introduced in Adelaide and helped to tip the balance by scoring 110 undefeated runs and taking eight for 52 in the match. In statistical terms it remains the best all-round debut in the history of the Ashes, and Trott must have had an exceptional talent, to clear the Lord's pavilion as he did playing for MCC against his countrymen four years later. His head, however, could not make the most of it. He was one of five players in this series to die before the age of 42. And one of three – along with Stoddart and Bruce, the first left-handed batsman Australia ever sent to England – to do so by his own hand.

AS AT THE BEGINNING of the series, Stoddart gave a look of despair after losing the toss in the final Test, having looked white as he had gone out to the middle. The pitch, reported the *Sydney Morning Herald*, was brown and "perfectly smooth, and as hard as flint". Giffen said to Ned Gregory, who like many Sydneysiders had come for the game: "Don't like those weeds growing in it." But the wiry sprouts of couch-grass had been forced right into the surface by prolonged rolling. Then the ritual took place again as the MCC (Melbourne version) secretary Major Wardill went into the Australian dressing-room to find out the identity of their captain. "I propose Giffen," said Harry Trott, Albert's elder brother and sort of senior pro. "I second," said Darling, and everyone shouted "carried". Giffen replied, "All right, lads, I'll thank you when I come in again", and went out to win the toss. He had been captain since Blackham's injury, yet still the democratic process had to be observed.

In compensation, Stoddart had Richardson, a 19th-century Angus Fraser with gypsy blood and swarthy face. In this deciding game he sent down 87.2 overs to take nine wickets and keep the Australian batsmen within bounds. The heat was so intense at times that the asphalted terraces surrounding the field were too hot to touch, flies troubled everyone, and 143F was registered in the sun. (Richardson must have been pretty strong just to maintain an over-rate of 22 per hour.)

As the game went on a wind blew up to help him bring the ball in from the off with his famous breakback. Yet this was no ignoramus toiling his heart out. In a chapter which he wrote about bowling – or at least had ghosted – Richardson talked of two types of yorker: the curling yorker, which swung or swerved into the right-hander and sounds like a forerunner of Waqar Younis's yorker, and the running-away yorker, which leaves the right-hander a little to hit his middle-and-off stumps. To be capable of both such deliveries argues for a high degree of technical sophistication, which was a Victorian speciality.

Most of the Australian batsmen made a start before being dismissed by Richardson or Peel, who bowled 94 overs for seven wickets. The second day attracted 29,900, the biggest crowd at a cricket match in Australia to date, but they did not see an Australian score a hundred, whereas Archie MacLaren made one for England, thus keeping the deficit down to 29. Excellent fielding by England, fuelled by their team spirit, stopped the Australians running away in their second innings, but the target was still 297, and the weather uncertain. While the MCG had covers, they could not be used once the game had begun. At the close of the fourth day England had reached 28 for one. The suspense for those waiting for the next telegraphed report must have been, in some cases, intense.

To the first ball of the fifth morning, from the leg-spinner Harry Trott, England's captain played back, missed and was given leg-before: it was only the fifth such decision of the series. The effect on England may have been similar to that of Graham Gooch's dismissal when he was dismissed in the first over of a day on the same ground a century later, before the crowd had settled. After clutching his left hand over his face all the way back to the pavilion, like Nasser Hussain after his innings of 94 against South Africa at Headingley last summer, Stoddart later had the presence to join Lady Hopetoun and to applaud the fine cricket of both sides with equal verve. Bookmakers had an England victory at 5-1, though they had no real precedent on which to base their judgment. Nothing like such a target had been achieved before in Test cricket (Australia's 199 for six in Sydney two years earlier had been the previous best).

The pitch was holding up alright. On the other hand, a report issued by the Observatory at 11.30 that morning had forecast fine weather for two hours, then squalls. Succeeding Stoddart was Jack Brown, the Yorkshire pro who was to hit two triple-hundreds in his career, and he seems to have been motivated to score what runs he could before the rain came to queer the pitch once and for all. A strong wind sprang up, blowing the Australian bowlers off course, and what is more, Brown began to bat like it. On the back foot he cut and pulled his way to 40 in 18 minutes, and to 50 in 23 minutes, so the local scorers recorded, making it still the fastest half-century in Tests. At the other end Ward was his consistent self, keeping his end up until the partnership was full steam ahead and he swung Giffen to leg for a five. Brown by now was using his feet to come down the wicket to drive the spinners straight, as well as glancing whenever the wind-hampered bowlers strayed down the legside. He reached 140 in 148 minutes, the same time as the partnership of 210, a new record for any wicket in Tests.

The Sportsman rated Brown's innings as "the finest performance ever witnessed on the cricket field" because of the "severe mental strain" under which it was played, as pressure was called in those days. Well before he had finished it was the Australian bowlers who were labouring under severe mental strain, without a fast bowler to use the wind as Richardson had done. Though Brown and Ward were both out before the end, another Yorkshireman and another Lancastrian in Peel and MacLaren took England to victory in the match by six wickets, and by three Tests to two in the first great Test series.

"The greatest match on record," wrote Brown in a letter home. "The excitement was intense." And it has never really abated since, except when the Ashes series have been too one-sided. ☾

MIKE BREALEY HEADINGLEY, JULY 1997

BILL O'REILLY ADELAIDE, NOVEMBER 1997

Stephen Brenkley

Typhoon Tyson

Stephen Brenkley, 45, is
cricket correspondent of *The
Independent on Sunday*. He still
plays most weeks for his village,
Harting in West Sussex.

Favourite Ashes innings
Tony Greig's 110 against Lillee
and Thomson in the first Test of
1974-75. A superbly defiant
exhibition – misleading as it
turned out in the context of the
series – but it made Greig the
Golden Boy.

**England have not won a
series in Australia since
the death of Andy Warhol
because...** Australia have spent
most of the intervening period
trying to produce enduring
cricketers rather than those who
might or might not be famous for
15 minutes.

On the voyage to Australia in the autumn

of 1954 the England captain took aside two of his young bowlers
for a private chat. He told them what they did not wish to hear: that
neither could expect to play a part in the imminent campaign to retain
the Ashes. They were, he said, in the party to learn and to provide
support on a long tour.

Len Hutton was half right. One of the players to hear his carefully
considerate tones in that meeting aboard the liner, *Orsova*, was
Peter Loader who was not selected in any of the five Test matches.
The half that Hutton got wrong was fairly spectacular. The other
member of the squad present at that meeting was Frank Tyson. He
did not spend the winter in quite the fashion outlined by his captain.

Tyson not only played throughout the series, he cut a swathe
through Australia's batsmen with bowling of imperishable speed and
ferocity. It brought him 28 wickets and a reputation which has
scarcely diminished down the years as the fastest bowler there ever
was. It earned him for all time the designation "Typhoon Tyson" and
those who were around to witness him maintained that it hardly
did him justice.

Tyson did not single-handedly win the rubber. He did not forget
at the time and he has never forgotten since the immense contribution
of Brian Statham and has invariably also mentioned the underrated
input of Trevor Bailey. Throughout riveting passages of play in three
consecutive Tests Tyson and Statham bowled together and together

they undermined Australia. If it was Tyson who took the majority of the wickets he was aware of the relentless, precise assault from his partner.

After his most compelling and rewarding exhibition in the third Test, which allowed England to take the lead in the series, the batsmen and the fielders prepared to applaud Tyson in. He had taken seven for 27, the last six of them in 51 balls. But he did not claim the glory exclusively. Instead he immediately shook Statham by the hand, linked arms and ensured they departed the arena together.

"Fast bowlers always have been at their best hunting in pairs," said Tyson on the eve of this winter's series. "I recognised it then and it still holds good. Brian Statham was one of the most wonderful bowlers and there was no let-up. He was unyieldingly accurate. In that series as a pair we were at the height of our physical and mental powers. It all came together so that we knew we had gained the psychological advantage over them."

Still, the series will forever be associated with the Typhoon more than with any other player. The raw speed and the haul of wickets it generated passed swiftly into legend but the ancillary details are quite as significant. There is the fact that he and England had to come from behind to win. The side were overwhelmed in the first Test, Tyson was mauled. The side regrouped, Tyson remodelled his approach in the space of two weeks. There is the nature of his rise. He came from nowhere to reach the pinnacle of his profession in six months. There is his demise. He was not to know such halcyon days again. He never played another full series; after that winter was done he won only 10 more caps spread over four years.

When his career was over and it was time to use his degree for a more conventional purpose (but who says fast bowlers do not have to be clever?) he emigrated to Australia. It has always seemed peculiar that both he and Harold Larwood, the two English speed scourges of Australia in Australia, should later make their home among them and be so accepted and so popular.

Tyson did more than that. He was offered a job as a teacher in Melbourne - yes, scene of his single most formidable return - which he accepted. A decade and a half later he became director of coaching in Victoria, a post he held for another decade and a half or so. He coached briefly in England afterwards. Throughout this time he wrote about the game intelligently, as you would expect, and his books include *The Century-Makers, The Test Within, The Cricket Coaching Manual* and an extremely singular dictionary called *Terms of the Game*. He has now retired to the sunshine of the Gold Coast where he occasionally passes on his vast cricketing knowledge – "only one-to-one, and only if I like 'em".

WHATEVER HUTTON'S PLANS for him, Tyson was a surprising and daring selection for the tour whatever Hutton's original plans for him. He had played barely 30 matches and in only one full season for Northamptonshire. His professional career began late. As a boy in Lancashire his speed gained him automatic attention and he was only 17 when a successful trial at Old Trafford led to the offer of a job on the groundstaff. He declined on the advice of his father because he was still at school and studying for the Higher Certificate.

On passing he was offered a place at Durham University but also had to do his National Service. He served his country first and then continued his studies. He was going on 22 when he had completed these obligations and then offered his services to Lancashire once more. He had played cricket in the Staffordshire League and for his university and his pace was a matter of some renown. But it was Lancashire's turn to decline.

Tyson alighted on Northants because he had met their Australian professionals, George Tribe and Jock Livingstone, during his league sojourn. They recommended him, Northants duly liked what they saw (or, more likely, considering the rate at which he bowled, what they could not see) and he was recruited. Before he could play for the county in the Championship it was necessary to serve a period of residential qualification.

He had one match for them in 1952, against the Indians. Having been subject already that season to the extreme pace of the young and menacing Fred Trueman, who had reduced them to nought for four on his international debut, the tourists could probably have done without Tyson. His first ball in first-class cricket swung so far that it reached first slip, who then proceeded with the rest of the cordon to retreat five yards. Later in the over Tyson dismissed Pankaj Roy,

The New Ball

bowled, as *Wisden* reported it, "by sheer pace".

The message and its messenger did not take long to get round. Midway through the following summer Tyson qualified but his first full season was in 1954. There is no question that on Northampton pitches which were not so much unresponsive as in a terminal coma he managed to find signs of life. To do so he adopted a run-up of some 27 metres and the county wicketkeeper, Keith Andrew, was some 60 metres away in all. It was above a newspaper photograph of this large gap that he first acquired his sobriquet. Referring to the distance and what could cover it in the blinking of an eye the headline read: "It Takes A Typhoon". How that was to stick.

The season still had a month to run when the party for the Ashes tour was announced in July ahead of the fourth and final Test of that year against Pakistan. Loader and Tyson were in, Trueman was not (nor, for that matter, were Jim Laker and Tony Lock, omitted for Jim McConnon and Johnny Wardle). The reaction was less incandescent than puzzled.

"I think I was surprised to be going," said Tyson. "There had been some speculation about it but I hadn't played many county games. The general reaction to the party as a whole was one of shock because while there were some longstanding England players it still seemed an experimental sort of side. It was pretty far-sighted of the selectors who seemed to be looking around for the nucleus of a side which would be around for five or six years.

"But there were a lot of bowlers around and a lot of comment especially about the omission of FS [Trueman]. I think it might have had something to do with the previous winter's tour to the West Indies. It hadn't gone very well at all and the word was that there had been some disagreement between Len and FS."

Having been nominated for the tour both Tyson and Loader were included in the side for the final Test against Pakistan at The Oval. There was no room for another part of the selectorial experiment, the 21-year-old Colin Cowdrey, who was made 12th man. Tyson took the new ball in both innings and took five wickets but Fazal Mahmood took 12 for Pakistan which won them the match. The defeat was unexpected but not cataclysmic. England's team had been picked with Australia in mind.

The *Orsova* docked in Perth on October 7 after the customary stop-over for a one-day match in Colombo. It should be noted that whatever the captain's plans for Tyson were at this stage, the bowler himself was fairly sure of the major weapon in his armoury. Surprised to be going he might have been, unprepared he was not.

"I had gained a reputation for being pretty quick and this is what the selectors had been looking for. If anybody asked me how quick I was I always said that they were putting the question to the wrong man. They should be asking the batsman, who was in the best position to judge. Or maybe the worst position. I realised that I could break through defences with my speed because batsmen somtimes weren't able to get their bat down in time."

No particular long-term strategy was plotted to cause the downfall of Australia though a short-term plan hatched on the eve of the first Test might have had catastrophic consequences. England began in sound enough form by winning the first three four-day matches. Tyson's five for 62 in the third of those confirmed his form. His accuracy and stamina both seemed greater than they had done the previous summer.

The match before the Test was against Queensland at the Gabba. It ended in a draw but it determined England's team. The pitch had been a greentop with enough moisture in it on the first morning to encourage the users of the new ball. Based on this evidence, England played four seamers and no specialist spinner. No England captain had won the toss and fielded in Australia since Johnny Douglas in 1911-12 when he led his team to an innings victory which regained the Ashes. Hutton won the toss and fielded. Australia made 601 for eight before they declared at lunch on the third day.

"Len often gets the blame for that," said Tyson. "But in truth he had no option but to put Australia in because of the strategy which had been worked out by the selectors. Our attack was all seamers and our best chance was likely to be on the first morning. It didn't work out like that.

"We dropped something like 12 catches and everything that could go wrong did go wrong. Alec Bedser wasn't fully match-fit because he'd had a really bad bout of shingles and was out of sorts all match. Our batting was weakened when Denis Compton ran into a barricade while he was fielding and broke a finger. It meant he wouldn't bat except in an emergency. It was then I realised what Test cricket was like. This was an alien evironment, different from anything I'd played in before."

Tyson bowled 29 overs and took one for 160. He had conceded 147 of them by the time he had Richie Benaud caught at cover point. He had worked up a head of steam but he was untidy. England lost by an innings and 154 runs.

It was then that Alf Gover stepped in and did his bit to transform the series, perhaps alter the course of history and help to ensure Tyson's place in the pantheon.

GOVER WAS REPORTING THE TOUR for *The People* but since his retirement as a player with Surrey seven years before he had established himself as a formidable coach. Players flocked to his indoor school in Wandsworth. Tyson had spent some time there both bowling and doing a little labour to build up his fitness levels. Gover knew his man and his action.

Tyson's long run somehow added to his menace. The distance between him and the wicketkeeper would have struck terror into the bravest heart and the most composed technique. It was a guaranteed indication to any batsman that he was about to face speed never before either generated or encountered. Maybe that was part of the reason for his adopting it but the other part was the County Ground at Northampton. The business part of its playing surface was bland and the longer Tyson ran in the more chance he had of achieving some bounce.

Gover told him to shorten his run, or, as the renowned coach was to put it later, "cutting out the first hop and starting from the second hop". By Gover's account this wisdom was imparted to Hutton and Tyson was not, at first, too happy about it. "Len told him that I was the one who knew and he'd better do it," Gover was to recall.

The transformation was achieved without much resistance according to Tyson. He knew he was operating on hard surfaces in temperatures he had never previously experienced, he had just taken one for 160, he was fighting for his Test place, he realised he had to do something. Gover reminded him that he had come off a much shorter run when he played in the leagues and at university. Tyson remembered it, too, and he remembered something else, something which seems quite astonishing.

"I've often said to people and got looks of disbelief that I think I bowled faster when I played league and university cricket than in profesional cricket. The reason I say that is I was bowling day in and day out as a pro, doing it six days a week." If that is so, anyone with a heart would send it out to the poor amateurs who had to face him.

What happened in Australia next was as quick and perpetually hostile as any observers could remember seeing. Tyson reduced his run by 12 metres to 15 but was utterly unconcerned that it would have any effect on his speed. It did not. "I did not have the most fluent of actions but I was strong and from the shorter run I was still able to achieve the necessary forward momentum."

There was one first-class match before the second Test in Sydney a few days before Christmas. Tyson came off the abbreviated run against Victoria in Melbourne and took six wickets in their first innings. It saved his place in the side. But there was still no specific plan to beat Australia. Hutton, said Tyson, let events take their course. Nevertheless the captain and the tour selectors made one sensational decision. They dropped Bedser. It was the first time in eight years that the stalwart seam bowler had been left out for reaons of poor form.

Tyson recalled that Bedser was not in good shape or form. The shingles had debilitated him. He was upset to be dropped but he was angry that he heard about it simply by not reading his name on the team list pinned up in the dressing room. Bedser and Hutton had gone through a lot together in four campaigns against Australia. The first three were failures but at last in the fourth in 1953 England had regained the Ashes. Bedser had taken 39 wickets. It cannot have been an easy decision for Hutton to go into battle without the willing old warrior but the decision, like so many more down the years, could and should have been handled more sensitively.

The second Test, when it arrived sans Alec, was as taut and as exciting as they can get. It was not the game which turned the series – it was too close, much too close for that, or anybody's comfort –

I think I

faster in

university

in profession

As a pro

six days

bowled
league and
cricket than
l cricket.
I was doing it
a week

but it gave England back their belief and respect. This time it was Australia's turn to put England in. There was some life in the wicket and England were all out for 154. Australia achieved a lead of 74. Tyson, not given the new ball, did not bowl as well as he might have done at the start of their innings, not well enough certainly to give a firm indication of what was to come. But he responded to the implorations of his captain by unleashing a combination of rapid yorkers interspersed with some choice bouncers and took four wickets.

When England batted for the second time, Peter May made his first hundred against Australia, taking nearly five virtuous hours over his 104; Tyson replaced him. More or less immediately he turned his back on a bouncer from Ray Lindwall and was felled. "I didn't know what had hit me, I was knocked out," he said. "There was some talk recently that I'd given some lessons to Ray about bowling bouncers and that this was the result. I really don't know where that came from. It's pure tosh. I had let Ray have a bouncer or two and he was letting me have some back, that's all." Tyson was led from the field but returned to resume his innings later.

Many years after this incident another England fast bowler, Devon Malcolm, was hit on the head while batting. He wore a helmet, of course, but the blow still provoked him to anger. He muttered to South Africa's fielders: "You guys are history" and soon after proceeded to produce the best bowling performance of his career and, with nine for 57, the sixth-best Test analysis of all time. Things were different in 1954. Frank Tyson was not wearing a helmet and nor did he have much hair to protect him. Though he was only 24 he was decidedly thin on top. If it occurred to him that the Australian guys were history he kept it to himself. But maybe, just maybe, it was the knock on the head which changed things so dramatically and not the shortened run-up.

He and Statham shared the new ball when Australia batted again. They needed 223 to win. "It was Statham and Appleyard that did it," said Tyson, somwhat mysteriously. "If they hadn't scored the runs they did for the last wicket in our second innings the whole thing might have been beyond us," he added by way of clearing up the matter. The pair had put on 46 with a mixture of the cavalier and the downright lucky. Going into the last day at 72 for two Australia were still favourites.

Now it was that Tyson started to enter the record books. After 45 minutes he took two wickets in rapid succession with balls to match. His yorker was swinging and at its most potent. He and Statham bowled extremely fast. It was thrilling stuff. Neil Harvey, batting at four, compiled an unbeaten 92, the innings of a craftsman, but the rest fell by the wayside. When Tyson had Bill Johnston caught down the leg side by Godfrey Evans England had won by 38 runs. The series was level.

ON THEN TO MELBOURNE REJUVENATED. Here the Englishmen seized the advantage and the initiative decisively and knew that Australia were incapable of regaining either. Here Tyson bowled one of the most incisive spells in all of Test history. It is said of him that he was so quick that those watching from the sidelines were often so startled that they gasped. Nowhere was that truer than at the MCG on January 5, 1955.

The game was riven by controversy. It was a dodgy pitch and the England innings was salvaged from wreckage only by Cowdrey's maiden Test century. He was to make 21 more but none was as lovely or heroic. His 102 came from a total of 191 (160 scored while he was at the wicket). Statham kept England in the match with five wickets and restricted the Australian lead to 40.

But on the rest day it seemed that the pitch was illegally watered. It had been breaking up and would, in all probability, have disintegrated by the fourth innings. England, said Tyson, were aghast. But they retrenched and set their opponents 240 to win after May made 91. Australia did not get close. The bounce was disconcertingly inconstant and in 80 minutes on the fifth morning Tyson dismantled them. It was dramatic stuff and Tyson knew then that he had them where he wanted them. Australia were broken.

"Len's tactics as captain were sometimes criticised but he was matchless when it came to the psychology of the game. And he knew that Australia had gone then. I felt it as well. I thought that we had finally worn them down. We knew how to get them out, most of them. They had never experienced pace like this against them and they didn't quite know how to react. There wasn't time for them to get adjusted to it. We had the edge and we knew how to get them out. Neil Harvey was somewhat resistant but early in the innings we felt we had a chance of getting him in the gully."

The fourth Test at Adelaide proved to be the decisive one. England were 2-1 up already and they won to move to 3-1 and an unassailable lead. How they won underlined the nature of their play and the way in which they had wrecked Australia's confidence. Although it got to be nerve-wrackingly close by the end it was once more high and irresistible pace which proved the trump.

The Australians, minus the injured Lindwall, perhaps vitally as events turned out, batted first and made 323. England replied with 341 and at last the captain made a substantial batting contribution for the first time. Hutton's innings of 80 was his first (and only) half-century of the series. By the last morning the pitch at the Adelaide Oval was crumbling and giving considerable assistance to spin in general and to Bob Appleyard's medium-pace off-breaks in particular. It was expected that he would form the basis of England's attack. Instead Hutton gave the ball to Tyson and Statham and never had occasion to take it back before lunch.

That decision exemplified Tyson's point about Hutton's instinctive awareness of the psychology of cricket. Sure, the pitch might favour spin but Hutton knew and Tyson and Statham knew and, above all the Australians knew that they were dangerously susceptible to speed. They were gone in the mind.

All morning Statham and Tyson bowled and for English observers it was a thing of beauty and passion. Together, this was perhaps their most celebrated few hours, their zenith. Individually, the figures were not spectacular but they were in perfect unison and they were on the verge of completing the job. Statham, rigorously accurate to the end, took the first three wickets to fall, Tyson the next three. For the second consecutive Test, Australia were bowled out in their second innings for 111. By now the home side were not only confronted with Tyson and Statham but with Nelson too.

England needed 94 to win and they had three hours and an extra day if necessary to do it. The latter was never likely to be required.

As it turned out the three hours remaining on the fifth day was almost plenty time enough for Australia to bowl England out. Perhaps shamed to some degree by their formless batting they made one last effort to take the contest to the final match.

"Len sat watching and as he did so he said, 'Oh no, they're going to do us again,' and for a while it looked as though those worst fears might come true," said Tyson. "The match shifted in an extraordinary fashion but Denis was there and he'd been through a lot against Australia as well."

Keith Miller found almost as much penetration as the English pace duo. By this time many of his countrymen believed that he, and not the luckless Ian Johnson, was the rightful captain of the side. Miller alone reduced England to 18 for three and that might have been 23 for four had May's attempted straight drive not dropped slightly short of the bowler. May hung around to help to add another 26 after his little alarm and in the context of the match, the series and the destiny of the great prize they were crucial. It was Miller who was reponsible for dismissing him, holding on at cover to a catch by his bootlaces.

Compton denied his chum Miller. It was not the vintage Compton, the sweeper and cutter of yore, but the quietly determined, mature version. He lost Bailey with a few runs to get but he saw it through with Evans, who made the winning hit.

"It was of course a magnificent moment," said Tyson. "We had done what we set out to do. It was the first time in 22 years that England had beaten Australia away. For some of the older members of the side it was a real apogee, the height of their career, because it was their last chance. To beat Australia in Australia must be the ultimate achievement for any English professional cricketer. I would say that to do it you have to raise your normal game by between 10 and 20 per cent and we managed to realise our ambition.

"These things go round and the Australian side was perhaps not as good as it once had been. They had come to England in 1948 and they had been given the title "The Invincibles". But they had got a bit older, a bit less useful. We had a different mix but it should not be forgotten that a lot of the same Australians went to the West Indies a few weeks later and did exceptionally well."

The New Ball

The fifth Test was ruined by the weather and was drawn. It mattered less to England and the weary Tyson because the job was already done. But their third young batting star, Tom Graveney, made an impeccable hundred. The Typhoon was the outstanding contributor to the series. In respect to his chief companion in the battle there was briefly a campaign to have him known as Sirocco Statham. It did not stick. It did not, after all, have quite the same ring because Sirocco did not have quite the same pace.

But Tyson was never again to be so propserous on a cricket pitch. He was dogged by injury, a stress fracture and a worrisome left knee to name but two. But it was a heel which gave him most pain and cause for concern. It was where he landed in the delivery stride and it curtailed his effectiveness. The doctors, it seemed, could do nothing. Only late in his career was the answer found. In Northampton, the home of shoe manufacturers, where the football team is known as the Cobblers, they developed for Tyson a heel glove. It worked like a dream, the pain was gone. But he had already made the decision to retire.

"It's often said that it was the injuries that made me go but it wasn't. I'd long since decided that I would retire from the game when I was 30. I had a degree and if I was going to make any use of it I knew I had to start another career. If I was going to be a teacher I had to begin teaching. There were people of my age who had already gone on to become deputy heads."

Before that there were brief excursions into international cricket once more. Twice he demonstrated to the South Africans that he was not to be messed with and when he was again named in the Ashes touring party for 1958-59 there was high expectation. Statham was there again and this time so were Trueman, Laker and Lock. The batting looked stunningly proficient. England lost 4-0. To this day Tyson is at a loss to explain why. It was the winter in which the controversy over throwing raged. Australia's Ian Meckiff was particularly supected. But England got on with the job. Tyson, as ever, paid gracious tribute to his old partner again.

"I couldn't get in the side because my form wasn't good enough early in the tour. By the time I did it was all over. But in the second match Statham bowled a truly majestic spell to make sure Australia didn't have too great an advantage. It was great fast bowling and it gave him seven wickets. Then Meckiff came on and threw England out. We were too polite, too courteous to make much of a fuss but it was obvious to me and it was so unfair to Statham's performance. Years later Meckiff was called but by then he was no more than medium pace."

But still that could not explain the size of the reversal. Tyson offered no more than that in that series it was Australia, led by Richie Benaud, who seized the psychological high ground. Benaud had been an ever-present but fairly peripheral figure in the 1954-55 series. He was some way from establishing himself as a key all-rounder as 10 wickets and a top score of 34 demonstrated. The player and strategist who confronted them four years later was a revelation to Tyson.

AFTER THE ASHES were safely ensnared in February, 1955 there was unfinished business for England. They had the New Zealand leg of the tour to undertake. This was a chore because it extended the tour but travelling by boat as they did it was the only sensible way to give New Zealand a game. England won both the Tests at a canter and Tyson and Statham, scourge of Australia, were far too much of a handful.

It surprised Tyson when Hutton expressed a desire to win the second Test by an innings because England were no more than 46 ahead. But they achieved the objective. New Zealand collapsed abjectly to 26 all out, still the lowest total in Test history. Tyson was removed from the atttack after taking two for 10 in seven overs ("much too expensive, I suppose") and Statham (three for nine) followed him not long after. But it was Hutton's intention to bring them back. The captain wanted his two series-winning bowlers to perform the final acts of the tour. Unfortunately for this plan, Appleyard rounded matters up before it could come to fruition by taking three wickets in four balls.

So Tyson was denied his finale. But this was a mere trifle. Six months earlier he had left England as a fast but untried bowler, of unknown calibre. Nobody knew what to expect. Tyson delivered in a way that Hutton aboard *SS Orsova* cannot have imagined and became a symbol of what brutal fast bowling can do. He still is. 🏏

GEOFF BOYCOTT MELBOURNE, MARCH 1992

DENNIS LILLEE LORD'S, 1997

Mark Steel

Behind Bodyline

Mark Steel fell hopelessly in love with cricket at the age of seven, and remains so despite supporting Kent. He spent several years as a stand-up comedian, has written and performed three series of *The Mark Steel Solution* and one of *The Mark Steel Revolution* for Radio 4, and the cricket documentary series *Mark Steel versus the MCC* for Radio 5. He also writes a weekly column for *The Guardian*. He can neither bat nor bowl.

Favourite Ashes innings
Jeff Thomson at Melbourne in 1982. With Allan Border he added 70 for the last wicket until, with four needed to win, he was caught shambolically at slip; drama no playwright could aspire to.

They usually get the better of us because... the population of Australia is one quarter of England's. The population of England which could overcome the social hurdles to become a cricketer, is one quarter of Australia's.

It could be "asshole", or "your mother's a whore",

or simply a gesture with a finger. But every culture has an agreement about the one thing which signifies that this argument will now become a fight. So that when it happens the surrounding chatter fizzles to a mutter followed by a dramatic silence, as everyone awaits the first blow. To the British ruling class in the days of the Empire that thing was the word "unsportsmanlike".

And in January 1933 Australian cricket's governing body, with the audacity of the barman in *Goodfellas* who says "Fuck you" to the psychotic gangster, sent a cable to the MCC, the MCC for christ's sake, about the English team's bowling, which read: "In our opinion it is unsportsmanlike, and unless stopped at once is likely to upset friendly relations existing between Australia and England." Until then the furore which surrounded the "Bodyline" series had been tense but containable, at the stage where nervous bystanders shuffled from foot to foot and muttered "leeeave it ... steady". But upon "unsportsmanlike", tables went flying and order was lost.

The MCC demanded that the word was withdrawn, the governments of both countries became involved, Australia threatened to leave the Empire altogether and J H (Jimmy) Thomas, Minister Responsible for the Empire, was to say at the end of his career that no other issue had caused him as much trouble as the Bodyline affair. The immediate cause was the tactic whereby the England captain Douglas Jardine packed his fielders on the leg side and ordered his fast bowlers, particularly Harold Larwood, to bowl short balls on the line of the batsman's body. But do Empires shake upon matters like this? Surely there was more to this episode than a row about cricket.

I FIRST READ about Bodyline as an obsessive teenage cricket fan in the Seventies, and was left confused. As part of my obsession I pledged to myself that I would read the entire collection of Swanley Library's cricket section, eager to learn about the history, the origins, and the characters behind the game, until about halfway through the 20th book it suddenly dawned on me that they were all completely fucking boring. Endless accounts of how many runs Patsy Hendren or Ranjitsinhji scored in an afternoon, which to anyone who wasn't there is as meaningless as an account of old lottery results. Or there was gushing prose about old players, which because great play can't be conveyed on the page seemed equally meaningless. So that my memory of these books is that they were full of passages like: "When Hobbs leaned forward to play a glorious cover drive at The Oval his follow-through was so graceful that women would faint and nearby mongrels would yelp in delight..."
One of the marvellous things about W G, these tomes would divulge, in language that could only have been written in a rural conservatory full of antiquated books which had never been read, is that he inspired the most splendid poetry. For example:

O to be in Gloucester
When Grace goes out to bat
146 not out and 4 for 36
My goodness. Fancy that.

I exaggerate, slightly. But where the majority of these books failed was in assuming that cricket was a world in itself. The immense upheavals which took place behind these matches would barely be mentioned. There may have been a world slump, the rise of Hitler and the Spanish Civil War but the only thing that mattered was Hammond's faultless back-foot technique. Cricket was immune to the tribulations of society. It was a refuge.

So in 1933 diplomatic relations between Britain and Australia were stretched to breaking point by a row about leg-side bowling. Typical is David Frith's book *The Fast Men*, which gives detailed accounts of the field placings and bowling strategy used in bodyline, but treats the episode as one relating solely to cricket. *The Oxford Companion to Australian Cricket*, a supposedly definitive 615-page compendium, makes no mention whatsoever of any non-cricketing tensions between the two countries. Yet bodyline/leg theory was used elsewhere without such enormous consequences. In his autobiography Larwood tells of how he first bowled in this way in a county match against Essex, but as far as we know there was no cable sent by Essex County Council to Nottingham Town Hall threatening to break off diplomatic relations.

THE STORY OF A WORLD POWER reaching a critical conflict with one of its major colonies only makes sense when seen as a reflection of tensions outside the sporting world. Yet ironically it's often conservative analysts of the game who insist on the link between cricket and one source of those tensions: nationalism. "If only players had the pride in their country that we had in our day..." they insist. But although Fred Trueman pursues this theory to the point of character comedy, there must be some link between a player and what his team stands for.

This link shouldn't be exaggerated. The courage and tenacity which may stem from collective pride can help to turn a war, but can only play a limited role in a game which depends on technique. Political determination enabled the Vietnamese to defeat the incomparably mightier American army, but that determination probably wouldn't have done them much good if they'd settled matters over a game of baseball.

However, if such a contest had taken place some things would have been transformed. The resilience of the underdog, the arrogance of the superpower and the tension in the crowd would all have been heightened somewhat. In the same way, it wasn't being an anti-imperialist that made Viv Richards a great batsman. But it did affect the manner of his greatness. The lolloping, menacing stroll to the wicket, the threatening grin, the panther-like posture, were all in direct contrast to the upright English demeanour. Certainly a team's results can affect the national character. The effect that the West Indies' first victory over England had on the independence movement in the Caribbean is well documented. As Trevor MacDonald has written: "West Indian success on cricket fields abroad, particularly in England, turned cricket into a positive expression of burgeoning West Indian nationalism." If we can beat the mother country at cricket, millions of people throughout the region thought, then we can surely govern ourselves.

The history of relations between the mother country and Australia wasn't quite as strained. Being transported for stealing bread or forming a trade union might be rough, but it had the edge on slavery. And many of the settlers who went as entrepreneurs felt they were planting the seeds of English fair play and democracy in another corner of the globe.

Australian culture developed in awe of the Britain the settlers had left behind. In 1869 the *Brisbane Courier* declared that the colonies' relationship to England was "that which a younger brother holds to a head of the family". This was reflected in the attitude to cricket. In 1880, as an English touring side arrived the Melbourne *Punch* upheld the tradition of awful cricket poetry with these lines:

Loving Old England with a child's affection
I'm to her fame and honour ever true,
But then my heart has formed a new connection
Hardly less strong – I love Victoria true
But through Old England we shall admire
The height to which they've brought their noble game
And our Victorians, vanquished, may acquire,
A knowledge which may lead them on to fame.

When the Australian team set off for England they declared their intention to "prove the colonials are worthy descendants of the good old stock from which they have come". Even the famous Australian victory at The Oval in 1882 led to statements that the result should make old England "proud of her descendants".

Australians wanted to beat England, not to get one over them, but to prove they were worthy Englishmen. "I can tell you sir," George Bonnor was reported to have replied to an insult from a spectator, "that I am as much an Englishmen as you or any gentleman present. I can trace my family back for six generations, and perhaps you can not do more." Few people would expect that response now when someone in the crowd shouts, "Warney you fat Aussie bastard", such a popular refrain in the summer of 1997.

But two things were transforming Australia. First, the growth of towns and industry was creating a vibrant labour movement; second, as the first world war approached, Britain's prime position in the world order was under threat, and its stance towards its colonies became more brutal. At this point Australia was yet to become a nation. The states had formed a federation "under the crown of the United Kingdom of Great Britain and Ireland". Australia had no flag, no national anthem and its coinage system copied that of Britain. In the 1896 Olympics Australian athletes had to compete as part of the British contingent. Elected officials could be dismissed by unelected ones from Britain. And if Britain so wished, Australia could be sent to war.

The turning point when Australia "became a nation" is usually thought of as the battle of Gallipoli, during which 7,818 ANZAC soldiers died in all-prepared attack on Turkey, as ordered by Churchill. But this creates two false impressions. Firstly, Gallipoli was only the most infamous episode of the war for Australians: 7,482 Australians would die at the battle of Bullecourt, and from July to November 1917 a total of 38,093 soldiers perished. Secondly, far from the experience uniting Australians, it divided every aspect of society along an irreconcilable line between rich and poor.

Two referendums were held on conscription, each resulting in rejection despite a massive campaign in favour from the press, industrialists, high-ranking officers and almost every politician. Tensions increased once the war was over when demobbed soldiers were left penniless, begging and often homeless. Most Australians now, if they still thought of themselves as a younger brother, must have thought they were part of a bitter family feud, with the rulers of their country as the elder brother, and Britain as a despised head of the family.

And if there was one institution which seemed to epitomise the arrogance and snobbery of the British, it was their cricket. This was a field in which class divisions were considered so sacred that players travelled in different compartments, changed in different rooms and walked onto the ground through different gates dependent on their status as amateur or professional. "Those of us who were at The Oval yesterday bore witness to the most appalling scene imaginable," attested one observer in 1921, "when the Surrey captain led his amateurs across the field to stand discussing and mingling with the professionals as if they were all of the same blood. At that moment we knew the spirit of Bolshevik Russia had invaded our game."

Perhaps the most blatant example of crackpot political ideas infiltrating cricket came when the English toured Australia in 1924-25. They were captained by Arthur Gilligan, who it was subsequently discovered was a member of the British Union of Fascists, and almost certainly used the tour to create branches of a fascist movement in the colony. If all Australians lived up to their stereotype the story from here would be simple. The whole country would have yelled "You Pommie Nazi poofters" at Gilligan's team, and the grand tradition of baiting the stuck-up English at cricket would have begun. In his book *Gilligan's Men*, however, Monty Noble, the former Australian captain, wrote that Gilligan was the "epitome of the English gentleman, a good sport of debonair countenance". I believe people said much the same about Himmler.

In fact the Gilligan tour was a great success, enjoying a friendly spirit and record receipts, but what can't be recorded are the subtle shifts in attitude that the Australian supporters had towards their opponents. The new contempt which working-class Australians had discovered for the British upper class can't have dissolved as fans poured into the grounds. And this shift was having some effect on the players. In 1926 Joe Darling, another ex-captain of Australia, wrote in his memoirs: "I have heard some English captains speak to their professionals like dogs." A few years before it would have been unheard-of for a prominent cricketer to talk with such disdain about an English captain. But the events which followed turned that disdain several notches further.

EARLY IN 1929 the Australian government informed Britain that it was in difficulty with two loans from British banks. These banks then exercised their authority to devalue the Australian dollar, with the Australian government having no say in the matter. The country went into a slump, with unemployment reaching 12 per cent. Employers demanded wage cuts from miners and dockers, provoking strikes. Sydney became packed with what the *Labour Daily* described as "ill-dressed, sad-eyed and gaunt-faced men collecting ration cards from the government bureau".

The government responded in two ways, restricting the meagre amount of welfare available, and asking to defer interest payments on a further loan from British banks. The British trade commissioner in Sydney advised the banks to take a harsher line than ever, forcing Australia to default on her payments, leaving her in a state of complete helplessness. "There seems to have been a decision by the British money markets, to put it bluntly," reported the London *Observer*, "that Australia should be taught a lesson."

Sir Otto Niemeyer was dispatched by the Bank of England to sort the Australians out. After a day dining in the finest restaurants in Melbourne, visiting the races and playing golf, he informed the Australian government that their citizens had been living "too luxuriously", and that wages and public spending must be reduced. The Australian government accepted the proposals so wages and pensions were cut by 20 per cent.

There was bitter resistance from the victims. Miners and dockers in New South Wales stayed out on strike for several months, despite being regularly attacked by the police. In January 1930 ex-servicemen formed a Labour Defence Army to defend the strikers. Following the attitude of British banks, particularly the speeches of Sir Otto, the battles in the labour movement took on a more strident anti-British character. The New South Wales Labour Party passed a law stipulating that Empire Day would no longer be celebrated and that schoolchildren would no longer salute the flag. The state premier, Jack Lang, stood for re-election in October 1930 on a platform of restoring wages, increasing public spending and if necessary repudiating interest payments to London. He won the election. The following year the Australian prime minister imposed

As a **political**
would serve
that Britain
no lengths in
rightful
world

tool Bodyline
as a reminder
would spare
claiming her
place in the
order

tariffs on British goods, and insisted on an Australian taking over as the new Governor-General.

In 1932 the British fired some decisive blows in retaliation. In May the British governor, an appointed viceroy called Sir Philip Game, dismissed Lang. It seems the people of New South Wales had democratically elected the wrong person, so they'd just have to democratically elect someone else. Five months later the Bodyline tour began.

MODERN SPORTSMEN AND WOMEN, when faced with the dilemma of the political world interfering with competition, are used to reciting the line "I'm not interested in politics, my job is just to win the race/match/fight." This was not a stance taken by Jardine. He was the son of the Advocate-General of Bombay, had been brought up in a Scottish mansion, and educated at Winchester and Oxford. He'd taken part in the 1928-29 tour, and been barracked for his habit of wearing a Harlequin cap and a cravat while fielding. In cricket as in society he believed passionately in the segregation of those who were born to rule and those who needed to be ruled.

Such a character was acutely aware of the political situation, and was in no doubt that the colony needed to be put in its place. The British authorities, in their political and cricketing forms, were well aware that Jardine was aware. The trade commissioner in Sydney had commented that the tour offered Britain an opportunity to bring Australia "back into the fold... more appreciative of the Imperial tie".

What was needed was an English captain who understood this, and who wouldn't flinch, on or off the field, from performing his Imperial duty; to leave the Australians in doubt as to their status in the natural order. Who better than a chap who wore a cravat in the outfield? Pelham Warner, the tour manager, said of Jardine: "He is a queer fellow. When he sees a cricket ground with an Australian on it, he goes mad."

The first stop was Tasmania, where Jardine was so rude to the locals that the Tasmanian President was pressurised into making an official complaint to the MCC. When the tour arrived in Adelaide, which was suffering unemployment rates of 30 per cent, 5,000 people turned up to watch the England team in the nets. Jardine summonsed the South Australian cricket secretary and insisted that they were all excluded from the ground. One day Jardine received an invitation to spend the day with one Major Alan Currie at his property, and duly attended with the team's amateurs, while the professionals, including Jack Hobbs, were left behind at the hotel. There was one amateur on the tour, however, who didn't quite warrant equal status. The Nawab of Pataudi was said by one correspondent to be treated by Jardine "with intense dislike... as if he was a disobedient native servant".

For such a man beating the Australians would be insufficient. That would only prove the English to be superior cricketers. They needed to be beaten in such a way that they would taste the wrath due to them for daring to challenge the status of their mother country.

And so the bodyline theory was born. As a cricketing tactic it could stop Don Bradman, the batting phenomenon disdainfully toppling every record there was. And as a political tool it would serve as a reminder that Britain would spare no lengths in claiming her rightful place in the world order. And if a colonial hero or two got a ball in the face en route, they'd just have to put up with it.

The first Test was in Sydney, where Jardine endeared himself to the local population with the sort of masterful public relations a New Labour spin doctor would be proud of. A journalist from an evening paper asked him who had been selected for the game, starting the next day, as his paper could then be the first to print the selection. Jardine's reply was: "What damned rot! We didn't come here to provide scoops for your or any other paper."

Bradman wasn't playing because of ill health, but during Australia's first innings Jardine signalled his fielders to move over to the leg-side in preparation for bodyline bowling. The tactic depended on Larwood, the Nottinghamshire miner who at that point was probably the fastest bowler in the world, and his ability to bowl consistently short and on the leg stump. Like an uncommissioned soldier he'd been informed of the plan by Jardine on a "need to know" basis, and was ready to carry out his duty, having practised the tactic for his county under the auspices of Arthur Carr. Etonian Gubby Allen refused to bowl bodyline, a decision which Larwood explains in his autobiography: "He could afford to do so – he was an amateur and not dependent on cricket for a living."

But there was another difference between Larwood and the amateurs. Although more than willing to bowl as ordered, and in no sense a radical, there was something in his background which ensured that he viewed the hostile crowd from a different perspective to his captain. "It was a time in Australia of dole queues, evictions, lines of jobless and a scramble for relief work," he wrote. "They needed a taste of honey. A man I came to know told me what he'd seen in a town called Captain's Flat in New South Wales. For every single job sixty or seventy men waited. The foreman would throw a pick handle high into the air and the man who emerged with it out of the wild scramble would get the job."

England won in Sydney, and Australia took the second Test in Melbourne thanks to a Bradman century. But it was in the third at Adelaide that the simmering hostility erupted into crisis. The details have almost become a mantra. Larwood bowls a short ball which thumps into the chest of Australia's devout Christian of a captain, Bill Woodfull, who slumps to the ground but resolves to continue. Just as Larwood prepares to embark on his next over, Jardine stops him and signals a bodyline field. The fielders move across and Larwood does his duty. Woodfull, clearly in pain, is subjected to a succession of short balls, many of which strike him until he is out for 22. While his injuries are being attended to in the changing room, he receives a visit from Pelham Warner, and is reported as saying: "There's only one team playing cricket out there..."

To a cravat-wearing fellow like Jardine, this sort of insult to England's good name was virtually a declaration of war. But the Australians became even more incensed when Bert Oldfield was struck on the head by Larwood, albeit when he wasn't bowling bodyline. Now the hostility reached a new level of intensity. Howling and barracking from the huge crowd threatened to become violent. The *Melbourne Herald* reported: "The atmosphere was electrical. Every time Larwood took up the ball a rumble of hooting began. It rose in a steady crescendo when he started his run...storms of hooting rent the air right through Larwood's over. The crowd, especially those in the outer grounds, were absolutely enraged." The outer grounds, we can be sure, were where the poorer supporters were seated.

"In all my experience of cricket," wrote Monty Noble, "I have never known such an atmosphere of such disgust and anger as prevailed this afternoon." English reserves and officials ran terrified to their changing room. "I'm getting out of here," yelled Maurice Tate, "somebody will get killed."

The crisis was reaching its peak. But was it really a row about cricket? Neither of the injured batsmen had been struck during the employment of bodyline tactics. And there have been countless other occasions in history when fast bowlers have damaged batsmen. Not that that stopped Jardine's popularity plummeting from its already sorry depths. *Truth*, a Melbourne magazine, said: "If there was a most popular man competition promoted in Australia at the moment and Douglas Robert Jardine constituted all three starters in it, it would be safe enough to wager that he wouldn't fill a place."

The New South Wales Cricket Association annual report stated that "this match aroused greater feeling than probably any other Test match ever played". Which became inarguable once the Australian Board of Cricket Control cabled the MCC with the protest accusing England of being unsportsmanlike. The MCC replied: "We deplore your Cable. We deprecate your opinion that there has been unsportsmanlike play..." Jardine then announced that he would refuse to allow his team to continue unless the word "unsportsmanlike" was withdrawn.

Does this make any sense if understood only within the confines of cricket? In diplomatic parlance "upsetting friendly relations" is the language of Foreign Office officials during a hostage crisis or border skirmish. Throughout his stance Jardine was backed by the MCC, who in today's parlance were thoroughly on-message about the political requirements of the issue. Conspiracies are usually hard to prove, but in this case there's pretty strong evidence that the MCC and the government were conferring to ensure they stuck to a united line; the President of the MCC was Viscount Hailsham who was also secretary of state for war. And JH Thomas was experiencing, if you remember, his most troublesome episode as Minister for the Dominions.

For Australia's part their government was fully aware of the fine line it had to tread, between remaining on wholesome terms with the mother country it was relying on for loans, and appearing to support the disdain its population held for that mother country. Eventually the Australian prime minister was informed that unless the key word was withdrawn, the banks would call in the Australian debts. Two days before the Brisbane Test the MCC received a cable which said: "We do not regard the sportsmanship of your team as being in question."

So the tour continued, along with bodyline, and England won the series by four matches to one. The shock tactics had restricted Bradman to an average of 56, which for him was extremely cheap.

TO THOSE WHO "only cricket know", the saga was an extraordinary, eccentric farce, in which cricketing passions reached such absurd proportions that heads of states were called upon to settle an argument about the legitimacy of a bowling strategy. But set against the background of immense social upheavals, every character in the drama played a logical and comprehensible role.

Imagine being one of those Australian spectators on a bench in the "outer ground" at Adelaide. You were probably brought up to feel as much pride in your English roots as your Australian ones. But almost certainly you lost at least one member of your family to a war fought over land you never knew existed. The reason, you'd have been told, was to pay your dues to the mother country. But then you'd have seen those dues repaid with unimaginable squalor.

The notion of life being tough but rewarding hard graft, handed down from your settler ancestors, must have been shattered. You'd have spent at least part of the last few years without work, and even while in work would have been surrounded by friends and family who, despite having the same willingness to work as ever, were denied that right. You'd have known someone up the street who as a result committed suicide, and have heard about once-proud drinking partners now begging on the same street. And you'd have been aware, from newspapers, leaflets, and meetings provided by the sizeable organisations of the labour movement, that the immediate cause was the determination of the British bankers and politicians to make the poorest section of society pay for a crisis they had no part in creating. And you'd have been profoundly aware of the tremendous resistance to that determination from miners, dockers and all those opposed to the culture of searching for that pick handle. And as the tour began you'd have noticed, as you were meant to, that a living caricature of the British ruling class had been selected to captain that mother country, to ensure that the ruthlessness of his Oxbridge contemporaries in other fields would be upheld on the cricket pitch.

But whereas in economic life the bankers and employers started with the in-built advantage conferred by wealth and power, on the cricket field you had Bradman, the most dominant batsman of his generation. So who can imagine the levels of anger running through your mind, as with great arrogance the advantage was restored by an apparent rewriting of the rules. In this context whether or not the bodyline tactics were formally legitimate in cricketing terms is almost irrelevant.

Social upheavals always have an immediate, and apparently trivial cause. The French Revolution began when a caretaker forgot the key to the Third Estate's meeting hall. The Russian Revolution was sparked by women working in a textile factory wanting to celebrate International Women's Day. But these were only the breaking points in conflicts which had been developing, sparking and threatening for generations. The immediate cause of the first world war was the assassination of an Austrian Archduke. But how many soldiers clambering out of their trenches over the next four years were thinking, as they hurled themselves forward, "This'll teach you to shoot poor Mr. Ferdinand, you bastards." In the appalling saga of human suffering that traversed the lives of working-class Australians from 1914 to 1933, bodyline was simply the last straw.

SOCIAL UPHEAVALS bring to the fore characters who are best suited to personify the role of the social classes competing in that upheaval. Supreme confidence, an unshakeable sense of duty, arrogance, a sense of destiny, and disgust for the lower orders: all these essential qualities of the British Empire were bound and parcelled in the personality of Douglas Jardine.

Jardine continued to antagonise the crowds, complaining that the Australian authorities weren't doing enough to control their citizens. "The total absence of any attempt on the part of the authorities to control their crowds and demonstrations," he asserted, "must give rise to a feeling that these performances have at least their tacit approval." Jardine's unflinching bile for the Australians was contrasted starkly with that of Larwood, who referred to the "great many comic remarks" which emanated from the crowd, and was particularly complimentary about the famously raucous supporters on the Sydney Hill. The different perspectives were reciprocated. Whereas Jardine remained a despised figure, Larwood was cheered by crowds once the tour had ended.

And what of the Australian authorities? They behaved in the classic fashion of leaders of a stifled nation. Like their counterparts in politics and industry, their pride was damaged by the manner in which the British brushed them aside. But they knew which way their bread was buttered, and would do anything to reach a compromise rather than unleash the forces from below, from whom they had far more to fear. Caught, not quite in the middle but certainly having to respond to the fury of the Australian public, they fired off their "unsportsmanlike" cable. But faced with calling the British bluff, jeopardising the tour (and its considerable profits) and possibly the Imperial tie, they backed down; just as they did to Sir Otto Niemeyer.

But one issue was still to be settled. In a bizarre and ironic aftermath, as Anglo-Australian politicians patched up their differences, it was considered that in order for the matter to be formally closed there should be one final apology, and that it should come from Larwood to the MCC. Larwood was informed of this by the well-connected former president of Nottinghamshire CC, Sir Julien Cahn, whom Larwood described as "a wealthy man, a Gentleman, a big businessman who rode in a chauffeured Rolls Royce". Larwood's reply was: "I'm an Englishman, I never apologise." Later he learned that the demand for the apology had stemmed from JH Thomas. The Empire was carrying out another of its favourite tricks; at the point of appearing to overstep the mark, protect the officer and sacrifice the private.

Larwood issued a statement in which he declared he was unrepentant, and wrote later: "In that declaration I locked myself out from Test match play for all time." He never played for England again. He moved to Blackpool and took no interest in cricket, except to watch one match at Old Trafford for which he queued and paid to get in. He bought a confectionery shop, saying: "You wouldn't find my name above the door. A recluse never advertises."

If it hadn't been for his interest in soccer, he said, he'd never have left the shop. His autobiography ends: "Nobody took a second look at the bespectacled man on Blackpool sands who sometimes bowled a rubber ball to the younger ones among his five daughters swinging a bat their father had carved for them out of an old piece of boxwood." Nevertheless, during Bradman's farewell tour of 1948, Jack Fingleton, one of his targets 15 years earlier, came into the shop. The pair had been corresponding for years and Fingleton was left under no illusions as to his ex-assailant's state of mind. "Larwood was living in almost complete obscurity," he noted in his diary. "Disillusioned, felt unwanted … could not be induced to talk of cricket." In 1953 Larwood decided to move his family to Australia, cabling Fingleton as he left London to request help with accomodation and jobs. Fingleton had a few words in some prominent ears and Larwood remained Down Under for the rest of his days.

GO TO AN ASHES TEST TODAY and you'll see gaggles of Australian spectators bantering with their English counterparts, cheering as bare-chested and sunburned friends return to their seats delicately balancing plastic towers full of lager past twisting legs. A few yards away sits an orderly line of sweltering men in suits and ties that seem welded to their bodies. As they politely acknowledge a thunderous boundary with soulless applause they appear to look down on the rabble below with the air of a Soviet Politburo at an old Russian rally.

The rabble and suits watch the same play from their different perspectives, probably unaware of the history and complexities of the separate traditions they stand in. But on the occasions when they catch each other's eye, they are all, in their own way, aware that they are they and we are us. 🏐

COLIN INGLEBY-MACKENZIE

MCC PRESIDENT, LONG ROOM, LORD'S, JUNE 1997

MIKE MARQUSEE

MARXIST WRITER, LORD'S, JUNE 1997

Ian Chappell

My Favourite Pom

Ian Chappell has done more than most to change the face of cricket Down Under. Born in Adelaide and a member of one of the game's most formidable clans – uncle Vic Richardson and brothers Greg and Trevor all played for Australia – he led his country in 30 Tests (1971-76), overseeing 15 victories and only five losses; in seven series he was unbeaten, winning five. Characterised by Richie Benaud as "rugged and ebullient", he totted up 5345 runs at 42.42 in his 76 Tests (1964-65 to 1979-80), four of his 14 centuries coming against the Pom. Forceful, imaginative and a prime mover in World Series Cricket, he has since turned to commentary and journalism with distinction.

Favourite Ashes innings
Doug Walters' century between tea and stumps at the WACA 1974-75. Having to hit a six off the last ball to complete both the century and the hundred in the session, and doing precisely that, captured all the daring of Dashing Doug's batting in one ball.

Australia rule the roost because... they are more consistent in batting, have a well-balanced attack and they are better and more athletic in the field. They are also mentally tougher than England.

At first, I must admit to being surprised when I was asked to write about my favourite Englishman. Then I thought, well, it could have been worse. I could've been asked to nominate my favourite Martian. That would have narrowed the choice slightly.

Then a strange thing happened: many names came to mind. I thought about Ian Wooldridge, the brilliant sportswriter and Royalist who first heard of his impending MBE in the house of an Australian Republican. However, Woolers ruled himself out by writing a book titled *Travelling Reserve*. I felt my choice must at least be a member of the first eleven, even if Wooldridge did have the advantage of not being an egg yolk and ketchup tie-wearing member of the MCC.

I tossed around the name Colin Milburn, that heavyweight hitter and renowned quaffer of pints, who once scored 180 off his own bat in a two-hour session of a Sheffield Shield match. Eventually though, even the name became so heavy after tossing it around for a while, that I dropped it.

Then there was a man of similar disposition to Milburn on the cricket field, the ultra-aggressive Basil D'Oliveira. D'Oliveira was forced to leave his own country to play international cricket, purely on the basis of his colour, and no-one fought harder for his adopted nation than Basil. Dolly was actually dropped off my bowling early in his innings in 1968 at The Oval and went on to make 158. That is one catch I don't regret going down because in hindsight, Basil's subsequent inclusion in the England touring party caused such a furore in South Africa it probably contributed to the situation changing in the Republic, albeit rather slowly.

I even considered the boys from Rammy, better known as the Ramsbottom Lancashire League team, where I was the pro in 1963. However, as much as Terry Stewart, Dally Brooks, Henry Hall et al, were household names in the main street of Olcombe Bruuk, their fame didn't spread as far as Headingley, never mind the Adelaide Oval.

The names kept coming, some surprisingly high on the list of priority. For example Ken Barrington, that Union Jack-carrying member of the batting line-up, from the days when dismissing an England team meant two days' hard slog, not two hours. Kenny was a difficult opponent to dislodge and former Australian wicketkeeper Wally Grout used to say, "Whenever I see Ken coming to the wicket, I imagine the Union Jack fluttering behind him".

However, I didn't consider nominating Barrington for his extended occupation of the crease or his occasional bursts of defiant aggression that three times saw him bring up a Test century with a six, which is triple the number of times he was dropped from the England side for slow scoring. So why did I consider him?

Well, such is the intensity of an Ashes Test that it is a surprise – nay a shock – when a member of the opposition offers some guidance. Kenny gave me some friendly advice at Lord's in 1972 – albeit after he'd retired – and it helped me immensely, although not in the manner it was intended.

At the time, I was a tormented batsman, having stupidly listened to ill-considered advice to give up hooking. Consequently, I wasn't sure whether to hook or duck and was doing, what a journalist once wryly observed about New Zealander Bob Cunis, that his bowling was like his name: neither one thing, nor the other. After the 1970-71 series against England I decided to work on my hook shot in order to play it better and reduce the risk of dismissal. This worked brilliantly for three months in the nets at a local school, but in the cold hard atmosphere of a Test match, the ploy came unstuck.

In the opening Test of 1972 at Old Trafford, the first ball I received resulted in the best hook shot of my career. Unfortunately it was caught at fine-leg by former England captain Mike Smith, and to cap an altogether inglorious innings the bowler was Tony Greig. He still constantly reminds me that my downfall was the result of precise planning. That wasn't the impression I gained from the England captain, who at the time was fielding at cover. As I wandered disconsolately past Raymond Illingworth, he muttered with typically blunt Yorkshire humour, "Fookin' good shot for nowt, suun."

Worse was to come. That night at Old Trafford I was ushered into the Australian trade commission tent by the commissionaire, who was nicknamed Wag, only to be confronted by a clown who accused me of being stupid because I'd fallen for such an obvious trap. After considering the merits of an uppercut to his jaw, I refrained on the basis that I'd never thrown one in my life and would probably miss. Anyway, our extremely perceptive manager Ray Castor Steele had hold of my right arm and was guiding me gently towards the bar. So it was Castor who had to endure my complaint that the only stupidity on my part was not getting more elevation in the shot. This, I explained, would have seen the ball land on the 12:45 bound for Oldham which at the time was departing Warwick Road station.

As I said, worse was to come. In the second innings, two balls after I'd had a between-over chat with my batting partner and vice-captain Keith Stackpole and told him, "if we see it out 'til stumps we can win this match tomorrow", I was again out hooking.

John Snow bowled a bouncer. I went for the hook and was given out caught behind by Tommy Spencer, despite the fact that when I looked at the umpire for the decision, my baggy green cap was askew after the peak had been hit by the ball. As I trudged off, there were no comforting words from the opposition skipper this time and I was left to contemplate the saying of a mate of mine: "They haven't got room in the scorebook to write a short story, only the result." My result read: Chappell I c Knott b Snow 7.

Unfortunately, scorebooks aren't standard issue for grandmothers, but in those days an aerogramme wasn't hard to come by. I received one from Dorothy Chappell, who knew absolutely nothing about cricket, a week later. At least Gran had the courtesy to ask how I was enjoying the tour before she came to the point. "Dear, a lot of commentators are saying you should give up hooking," she wrote. "Maybe you should consider it."

That was it, I decided. A man could only take so much. The day after we'd lost the Old Trafford Test, the Combined Universities' opening attack, a couple of medium-pacers named Spencer and Hadley, had both bowled with two men back at fine-leg in an attempt to trap me on the hook shot. Then the letter from Dorothy arrived. I was mad as hell and I was going to hook. Well, I was almost certain I was going to hook in the second Test at Lord's.

As a last-minute preparation I had Jeff Hammond pepper me with short-pitched deliveries in the Nursery End nets the day before the game. Even that became an ordeal. "Now your own bowlers think you're susceptible to the bouncer," one fan chirpily informed me from behind the net. Still, I'd survived the exercise and was ready to hook whatever the English bowlers bounced at me.

The next day we fielded while Bob Massie humbled the English batsmen. By the time it was our turn to bat on the second day, my steely resolve to hook had diminished somewhat. That is when Ken Barrington appeared in the Australian dressing-room.

I was padded up and sitting in the corner of the room watching through a small rectangular window as Stackpole and Bruce Francis negotiated the opening overs. Barrington slid into the seat next to me and followed a smiling "hello" with, "Ian, perhaps it would be best if you avoided the hook shot", then, as an afterthought, added, "at least until you have fifty on the board".

I had to look twice to see if Kenny was taking the mickey, but I knew that wasn't his style, so I thanked him for the advice and turned to watch the game. That's it, I thought as Barrington walked out of the room. When an Englishman tells me to shelve the hook shot, it's definitely time to play it.

Francis was soon out to Snow bowling from the Nursery End and I walked out to bat confident I was going to hook. However, in the heat of the battle I wavered and Snowy's first short one hit me in the ribs as I was again in no man's land, thinking, "will I or won't I?"

The sharp pain in my left side finally cleared my mind and for the first time in a couple of years I let my instincts take over. I hooked everything that Snow and John Price hurled at me and even though

I was finally out hooking, again caught by Smith at fine-leg, the bulk of my 56 runs had come from that one shot.

It was an important knock for both the team and myself and I've always regarded it highly, because it proved to be a watershed in my career.

That is why, like WC Fields, who once said, "A woman drove me to drink and I never even had the courtesy to thank her", I have pangs of remorse, because I never thanked Ken for the role he played in my rehabilitation.

IT'S IRONIC that John Snow also had a hand in convincing me I was right to continue playing the hook shot. He was the bowler responsible for me getting into a tangle back in 1970-71 when I was in a dither over whether to play the shot or ignore the short-pitched ball. Snowy wrote some poetry in his spare time and he once said about the bouncer: "(It's) a short and emphatic examination paper that you put to the batsman."

I felt I passed the exam that day at Lord's (any one of my schoolteachers would have considered a 56 from me as conclusive evidence of cheating) and continued to improve following further searching tests. Every day against Snow was a tough examination as he was the best pace bowler I played against. Like all really good bowlers he produced a new weapon each series you played and he seemed to save his best for Australia.

I was once asked by a radio interviewer who had Snow on the other end of a three-way line: "What did you say to each other out in the middle?" I answered: "There was never one word that passed between John Snow and myself out in the middle during all the Ashes battles we fought." John confirmed that this was the case.

I won't say I was never guilty of saying anything on the cricket field and sometimes what I said couldn't be classed as gamesmanship, which I believe is a legitimate part of the game. However, I can assure you very little was said on the Test match field because most cricketers at that level work on the theory that you never upset a good player because it will only make him more determined to succeed.

When Snow was surprisingly (to all Australians) left out of the England side to tour in 1974-75, he was asked by a Melbourne

The thing Gatting was to ignore He avoided gaze and doing his

smartest
did in 1986-87
Ian Botham.
Botham's
went about
the job
way

newspaper to go through the weaknesses and strengths of our team. In writing the article John mentioned that everytime he bowled a bouncer at one Australian, the batsman in question mouthed an obscenity at him. A lot of people assumed it was me, which I resignedly put down to the adage about giving a dog a bad name, but little did they know it was the most unlikely candidate in our side.

As you have probably sensed by now, it annoys me that a lot of ill-informed people blame me for supposedly initiating the ploy of abusing opponents on the cricket field. Whilst I don't claim to be totally innocent, as I always believed in responding to anything that was said to me on the field, I would like these points to be considered in my defence.

Firstly, it is said that this tactic was devised to unsettle opponents. Well, as captain I had great faith in my teammates' ability to dismiss batsmen thanks to skilful bowling. I also felt that bowlers like Dennis Lillee and Jeff Thomson didn't need any help when it came to the unsettling process.

Secondly, if teams under my leadership were so badly behaved how come not one Australian player was even reported during my captaincy tenure? If all this shouting of abuse was going on, especially as is claimed in the 1974-75 period, I, for one, would have been at least 20 metres from the batsman on most occasions, standing in the slips for Lillee or Thomson. Don't you think umpires of the calibre of England's Dickie Bird and the stern disposition of Australia's Tom Brooks would have stepped in to stop such abuse?

"Ian had very firm views on the way the game should be played," Mike Brearley once said. He's right, and I believe that is from whence a lot of the trouble stemmed. If, for instance, I felt an opposition player was scowling at us for appealing, I would leave him in no doubt that it was his job to bat, ours to appeal and the umpires' to issue a verdict. I would then inform him that we'd all get on famously if it remained that way. As I do tend to swear occasionally, these little dissertations were often spiced with the odd four-letter word. I'm sure some players thought this was an attempt to unsettle them, but my sole intention was to defend Australia's right to appeal when we thought a batsman was out.

I always felt that a defect in a player's character was there to be exploited, in exactly the same manner as happens with a weakness outside off stump or against the short-pitched ball. There is a place in cricket for gamesmanship. It has been recorded at least as far back as Dr WG Grace, and much of the humour from the game that is written and spoken about has resulted from such thoughtful needling. On the other hand, umpires should report mindless abuse if their warnings aren't heeded and the offenders should then be punished.

PUNISHMENT WAS something that I rarely dealt out to another highly competitive Englishman. "Deadly" Derek Underwood was well named, as I had a tougher time scoring off him than any other spinner I faced. I recall running into Deadly at the Cricketers' Club in Baker Street during the 1977 tour. He was playing and as I'd recently retired, I was covering the tour for an Australian newspaper. We had both signed to play World Series Cricket (WSC) and with news of Kerry Packer's audacious venture having just broken, we felt comfortable broaching the subject as we shared a cab to the West End.

"Well, Deadly, it looks like our contests have been revived," I remarked.

"Yes," he replied, "just when I thought I'd seen the last of that damn broom."

His reference was to my sweep shot, which was one of the few available to a right-hander against his deadly accurate, quickish left-arm orthodox spin. I knew the shot irked Derek out in the middle, but he could always joke about it over a beer afterwards. However, on pitches like the fuserium fungus-affected one at Headingley in 1972, even the sweep shot was nigh impossible against him. On anything slightly damp or soft as Headingley was on that occasion, he would bowl the occasional Superman ball – up, up and away. These deliveries would turn and bounce, making scoring for a right-hander difficult and keeping wicket a nightmare, not that you'd ever have known from watching Alan Knott at work.

The eccentric little gloveman was one of the best and in situations like Headingley he excelled. Knott was also a great contributor with the bat, facing up French-cricket style and then sweeping and cutting the spinners and driving the fast men crazy with his innovative strokeplay. In the final Test of 1972 at The Oval, we were pushing hard for a series-levelling victory and Knotty was the bane of my life, scoring heavily in both innings. Every time Massie bowled an inswinger Knott would hit it over midwicket, no matter where it was pitched, almost as though he was doing it purely to let the bowler know that he was detecting the direction of the swing early. Even though I knew placing a fielder on the midwicket boundary for a fast bowler was virtually capitulating, I thought seriously about it on a few occasions.

The great improvement shown by Rod Marsh after his first series in 1970-71 made the wicketkeeping duels in the next three series – through to 1975 – an aficionado's dream. Knott and Marsh both kept brilliantly and played a number of important innings when runs were needed. I reckon those two often cancelled each other out as their performances were on a par and that says volumes for Rodney's dedication to improve after a shaky start to his career.

Mention of the Headingley fiasco in 1972 is a vital clue as to why I haven't included any administrators on my list of favourite Englishmen. The tendency for groundsmen in England to make pitches to instructions is something I think should be stamped out. I've harboured this opinion ever since I asked that loveable rascal Bert Flack in 1963: "What was the pitch like that you prepared at Old Trafford in 1956?"

"T'were a bluudy bad 'un," replied a grinning Bert. " 'Eadquarters told me to prepare a bleedin' turner," he continued, this time breaking into laughter, "and a bleedin' turner t'were." From that moment on I was a fan of Bert's, appreciating his straightforward honesty and later discovering his spirited sense of humour over a pint of his favourite brew. It still irked me when I read in 1995 that as captain, Mike Atherton was cranky with the Edgbaston groundsman for not preparing a pitch to help England rather than one that suited the West Indies' pace bowlers. Surely the square is the sole domain of the groundsman/curator and if he makes a botch of the job then he's sacked, but he shouldn't be told what type of pitch to prepare. The fact that this habit is still being encouraged rather than discouraged in England is a black mark against the administrators.

Despite Atherton's outcry I admire the former captain's approach to the game and apart from their long-term association with Lancashire, he and Flack have a lot in common, not least their sense of humour.

At Edgbaston in 1993, I was enjoying a glass of red and a chat over old times with the former England fast bowler David Brown and some of his horse-racing friends. We were standing around on the edge of the second XI field when Atherton, who had just taken over the captaincy from Graham Gooch, joined the group. He told me that England's coach Keith Fletcher had been discussing the pace of Lillee and Thomson in the Seventies and by way of example he said that Thommo had hit him in the head at the SCG. "Is it true," asked Atherton, "that the ball hit Fletch flush on the cap?"

"Right on the England badge," I replied, "but not flush. It flicked his glove on the way through and if Roscoe (Edwards) hadn't been so worried about Fletcher being hurt, he'd have caught the ball at cover."

Atherton gave me a quizzical look and said: "Since when did Australian cricketers worry about the well-being of Englishmen?"

It was easy to understand Michael's point of view, as at the time he was deep into a six-Test series where he'd batted for long periods against Merv Hughes. Nevertheless, with his ready wit and calm logic I don't think Atherton has to worry about too many fast bowlers getting the better of him in a verbal joust. In fact, when Michael looks back I think he'll find, like most of us who have done battle in Ashes series, that Rodney Marsh was right. "Adventure," he once told me (although he now doesn't recall passing on the quote), "is discomfort remembered in tranquillity."

The fact that this statement applies equally to the game of cricket as it does to life, perhaps has something to do with the length of opposing fast bowlers' conversations being inversely related to their pace. I found this to be particularly true in the case of Snow and Peter Pollock. I recall having a night out with the elder Pollock brother in 1970 and asking what had brought about the remarkable change? "You were an ignoramus in 1966-67," I apprehensively suggested, "just grunting at any greeting – and now you're out drinking with the opposition."

"I've discovered that there are friends to be made in this game," said Peter. "I just hope I haven't left it too late."

Similarly, I was more likely to engage in a conversation with Snowy after a day's play in 1975 than in 1968. This is an accepted part of cricketing life, unlike the fact that I still owe John a beer from a night where we ran into each other in Barbados and stopped at a sidewalk bar. I hate being in debt to anybody, but especially a fast bowler.

Peter Pollock was right, even if he did discover it late in his playing life: there are friends to be made in cricket. And so often it is the fiercest of adversaries who become the closest acquaintances when their playing days are over. There is a simple explanation for that phenomenon: it is called respect. It's a deep-down, begrudging respect while you're still playing, but it usually blossoms once you retire to an atmosphere devoid of conflict and the need to win.

A former Prime Minister of Australia, Sir Robert Menzies, said many years ago: "Great Britain and Australia are of the same blood and allegiance and history and instinctive mental processes. We know each other so well that, thank heavens, we don't have to be too tactful with each other."

Although both societies have changed markedly since he made that comment, Menzies' observation still strikes right to the heart of Ashes contests. Apart from the tradition that precedes every Australia versus England series, the point made by Menzies is the reason why both players and fans still keenly anticipate these battles. Even though Australia has been the dominant team since 1989 and England has not been a real force in the game since the Ashes series of 1972, these battles still loom large on the cricketing calendar of both countries.

A major difference between the two countries is best outlined by the varied reaction of the respective authorities in times of desperation. Australia were in a bad way in the Eighties, having lost disastrously in 1981, 1985 and again in 1986-87. At that point Australian cricket took some drastic steps to turn things around, the most important being a selection policy to choose players with character as well as skill. As often happens with Australian cricket, because of the tendency to take the aggressive rather than the negative option, the turnaround followed quickly.

In England's case there is still a "we rule the world" mentality in sections of their cricket. Consequently there's never been a full-throated admission that England is playing crap. Until such an admission is made, it is impossible to fix the problem properly and only band-aid solutions are applied. In this case, Australia's honest and forthright admission served it well, while England's stiff-upper-lip approach has elongated the healing process.

The old enemy's last period of Ashes domination, the mid-Eighties, was highlighted by the best England captaincy I've seen since Illingworth. I learnt a lot about captaincy from the gritty Yorkshireman, especially in the most difficult art confronting a skipper. As a captain, Illy was a master at sending out the signal that he was still searching for a wicket even when he knew saving runs was of vital importance. I enjoyed doing battle with Raymond and contrary to some rumours, never an angry word was exchanged between the two of us. I regard it as a privilege to have come up against Ray at the commencement of my captaincy career as it helped to shape my attitude to the job. After Illingworth, Mike Gatting is the best skipper I've seen from England.

The smartest thing Gatting did on the 1986-87 tour of Australia was to ignore Ian Botham. The burly all-rounder was responsible for spearheading some marvellous England victories in the 1981 series, but he had two bad habits on the field. As a bowler he wanted a man everywhere the ball was hit and he was also prone to moving fieldsmen even though his time as skipper was past. In these moments Gatting avoided Botham's gaze and went about doing the job his way. His way was very successful on that Australian tour and yet his most audacious move as a captain came in the only Test England lost.

Australia was on top at the SCG and seemingly headed for a comfortable victory. Allan Border was enjoying the rare luxury of having fieldsmen crowded around the bat and at 102-5 chasing 320, England's remaining hope appeared to be in hanging on for a draw. Defying most of the books written in England on cricket tactics, Gatting decided to launch a counter-attack. This move proved so successful that Border spread his field to save runs, unsure whether his opposite number was bluffing or seriously going for victory.

It was a tactical masterstroke and Gatting complemented it with some glorious shot-making. He appeared to be successfully thwarting Australia's charge for victory when Steve Waugh had him caught and bowled for 96 and the game was eventually lost. Sometimes good or bad captaincy can't be judged simply by looking at who won and who lost. There are times when the manner in which the game was played counts for something and that day at the SCG Gatting was at his best as a leader.

I enjoyed Mike's captaincy and I thought he was badly done by when – in criminal parlance – he was sent down. The officials might have blamed his loss of the captaincy on the barmaid affair, but in my book it was a throwback to the blow-up with umpire Shakoor Rana. The administrators of both sides, who had been unable or unwilling to sort out an escalating row that had simmered for years, exacerbated Gatting's problems in Pakistan. This was yet another case of a player getting it in the neck because of administrative negligence or incompetence.

DESPITE NUMEROUS off-field failings and a fast-changing world, the game endures. And despite the dominance of Australia in recent years the Ashes series are still eagerly anticipated, with sell-out days in England at almost every venue in 1997. Even so, we should never take the game for granted, as not everyone brought up in a cricket-playing country adores the game.

This point was driven home recently while I was reading *The Pick of Punch*. A piece by Robert Morley, titled Death to the Flannelled Fools, caught my eye and I decided to read why he wanted me, and others like me, to be erased.

In his article Morley states: "I would rather watch a man at his toilet than on a cricket field." I understand that not everybody is in love with the game of cricket. Nevertheless, I felt Morley was a little harsh in his observation, perhaps condemning the rest of us because he'd once had to endure watching Geoff Boycott bat.

I have great respect for many England cricketers and admire a lot of others. At different times I've enjoyed the company of many of those players and a lot of Englishmen who have never played, but nonetheless, wholeheartedly support Their Team. They and others like them would be encouraged by England's gradual improvement in the last couple of years, and in Alec Stewart they have a combative captain who can lead the way with his own aggressive brand of play.

Despite England's improved showing of late, no-one connected with the game in the country can rest until the team is once again a force in cricket. The international game needs a strong England side and not only should the aim be to reach that level once again, but also to then maintain the standard. Not so strong, I hasten to add, that they beat Australia regularly.

I always look upon an Ashes scoreline of 3-2 to the Kangaroo as having a pleasant ring to it. It is on such occasions that I have a lot of favourite Englishmen. Eleven immediately spring to mind. ❱

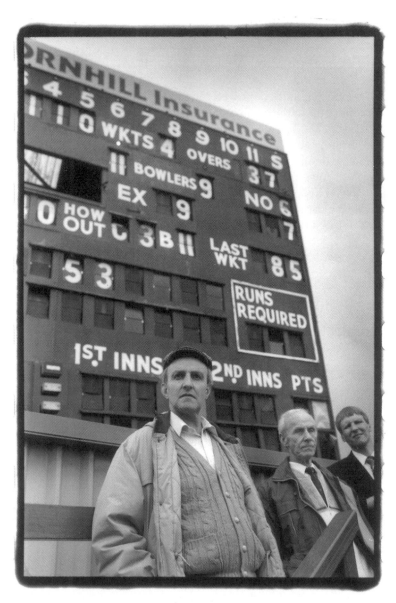

English supporters Old Trafford, July 1997

AUSTRALIAN FANS MCG, DECEMBER 1990

Dirk Wellham

No Poofters

Dirk Wellham was a schoolboy
prodigy whose century in the
sixth Test at The Oval in 1981
made him only the second man to
score a hundred on both his first-
class and Test debuts. An English
schoolteacher by trade, he averaged a disappointing 23.36 in his
six Tests, but compensated by
leading New South Wales to the
Sheffield Shield in 1984-85 and
1985-86, earning wide repute as
an astute tactician and subsequently becoming – for Tasmania
and Queensland – the first man to
captain three states in the Shield.
Described in the *Oxford
Companion to Australian Cricket*
as "a complex and sometimes
uncompromising character", he
retired in 1994 and made an
unsuccessful bid to run as the
Liberal candidate for the State
seat of Carlingford. *O My
Captain* is his second book, his
first being *Solid Knocks and
Second Thoughts* (Reed Books,
Sydney, 1989). He recently
completed a thesis on educational
leadership.

Favourite Ashes innings

Dean Jones' 184 not out at the
SCG in 1986-87. It was my only
home Test and I was enjoying
being out there with him for too
brief a time. He struggled early
then dominated the match in
inimitable Deano style.

Australia is traditionally and blatantly superior

because... we don't think technique, we think tough. If the ACB
dump Mark Taylor, we may not be
superior for long. He does think.

What better way is there for a man to get to know
another man than by playing a season of cricket with him, fielding
together for hours at a time, perhaps in close proximity in the slips?
Consider the marriage of opening batsmen. Bill Lawry and Bob
Simpson knew each other so intimately that when they ran together
they instinctively knew what the other was thinking, so they had
no need to communicate verbally. When opposing keepers get
together there is always a genuine, shared warmth of emotion that
radiates from their secret mutterings. The symbol of their trade, the
well-worn leather of their gloves, reveal a peculiar odour of animal,
rubber, perspiration, grime and a primal ingredient unique to their
calling. Umpires, usually former fast bowlers, stand together for
hours at a time, communicating by time-honoured hand signals
comfortably at home in this secret society. Why else does the game
take all day to play? Forging emotional links may take hours of subtle
communication. A captain's charge is to acknowledge them all.

Think of the emotions that are dragged out of players during a
match. Like any recreational activity, cricket is at least partly
designed to remove the individual from the stresses and strains of
normal life. In some case, the smell of a newly-mown field is sufficient
to spirit a player back to some other subliminal existence, to some
warm summer's day when the game was the thing and nothing else
mattered. There are no bills to pay on the meadow, no children to
consider, no deadlines to meet, no female code of manners and

etiquette to consider. There is certainly a moral code but it is a gentleman's code with no subtle female coquettishness. These morals relate more to frankness and openness with one's teammates, while allowing for subtlety and deception towards the opposition.

Cricket is a rather strange, English gentleman's game. Only gentlemen could dream up a game where you could play in earnest without actually having to do all that much. It is played by men who lock themselves away in dressing rooms or in the middle of a distant meadow. Yes, yes, I know there are excellent women's teams too, but I think they are a fairly recent, post-modernist phenomenon. I can't believe that when the lads decided that they'd like to separate themselves from the clutches of young women, that they ever envisaged there would be females having a bat and a bowl in the net next door, or having a celebratory lager in the club room.

So, if you accept that women playing the game was not the intended purpose of the gentlemen who devised cricket, then it follows that cricket is intended to allow men to experience the emotions of the game in private, affirming groups where one's character could be revealed, analysed, marvelled at, or even quietly ridiculed, securely without the questioning glare of the female, and in a rare male context that accepted the communication of feelings.

MALE BONDING, the latest euphemism for teamwork, has been positively reinforced in recent times, probably for a long time, in Australian cricket. It's interesting that the most successful teams in Australia, in the Eighties and Nineties, have been New South Wales and the Test team. Neither Bob Simpson, for so long the national coach, nor Mark Taylor are exactly blokes in the true Australian mythological, post-European settlement sense.

In December 1995, during Channel Nine's coverage of a Test match – against Pakistan or Sri Lanka, I can't quite recall – I heard Greg Chappell discussing the fine work being achieved by Rodney Marsh in Adelaide at the Australian Institute of Sport Cricket Academy. Perhaps Rodney is doing a great job. I have no way of knowing except by personal observation. The reality is that our best young cricketers have always grown older and more experienced and progressed into Sheffield Shield and Test teams.

The process now involves being nominated by your State Association as an 18- or 19-year-old, promising, first-class player of the future. On receiving an invitation to join the Academy squad a player faces the decision of accepting and moving away from family, friends, work, education and familiar cricket, to unfamiliar people, in a closed cricket environment, albeit for only a short period of time. The alternative is to politely decline and face the prospect of being labelled as not committed. Consequently, most recent young Shield players have gone through the Academy, where, presumably, they are coached intensively. For every "graduate" who is escalated into their Shield and perhaps Test team, I could name a failure, someone who didn't make it at Test level. Just as it has always been.

However, what particularly interests me was not Chappell's comments on what great cricketers Marsh's Academy turns out. As a way of further praising Rod's work, Greg said: "And they're not just turning out good cricketers. They're turning out good blokes too." One would assume that with the Academy turning out good blokes, courtesy of a great, well-known authority on what it takes to be a bloke, and having such praise broadcast to a watching nation by a great Test batsman and ex-Australia captain, the notion of the need to be a bloke is well entrenched in our cricket.

The case of that other squat giant of a bloke of recent vintage, David Boon, is an interesting one. Boon established himself in the Australian team under Allan Border, who modelled his own captaincy on that of his Queensland mentor, Greg Chappell. AB built a reputation, apart from being a brilliant player, as a Good Captain and One Of The Boys. Most people regard him as a Good Bloke, hard but fair. David was a tremendous batsman for Australia throughout his distinguished career, but once Mark Taylor inherited the captaincy, he struggled against Pakistan and West Indies, and retired soon after.

David Boon gained a modicum of notoriety for breaking the record for the number of cans of beer consumed on a flight between Melbourne and Heathrow, previously shared by Doug Walters and Rod Marsh. With the rise of professionalism in world cricket Boon may well still hold the record when Australia collides with Asia. Were his moderate Test performances in his final years a sign of ageing?

He'd taken to wearing glasses off the field: was he worried about his eyesight? Or was it simply that he lost the comfort of being around Blokes such as AB and Geoff Marsh?

Boon's last Test team was led by a Non-Bloke. Simpson had certainly never been one. The Waughs are one of a kind (if twins can achieve that status). Michael Slater is an enthusiast. Ian Healy is A Bit of A Bloke, being a good mate of AB's. Paul Reiffel, Glenn McGrath and Craig McDermott just aren't in the same league as Rod, Doug or David, in terms of Blokedom. It made me wonder whether Boonie was starting to feel a little isolated. Perhaps he didn't have quite the same security as he had with his closest mates around him.

Then there were the youngsters, the Slaters and Laws, Pontings and Blewetts, beginning to make him fret, make him worry that he was getting on a bit. They always distracted him with their athletic fielding, their enthusiasm, their self-contained courage and confidence. And, perhaps more importantly, their youth. They provided no motivation, only threats and ostracism. Doubts about his own desire created inner fear. The youngsters added immediate fear, that if he did not succeed he would fail, totally. Once the doubts start eating away, the hands tense and the mind says: Look out – this might be the late, nipping leg-cutter. Did you see the way he looked at you? Did you see the change of grip? Did he drop that left shoulder a little more that time?

BLOKES HAVE MADE great players in Australia, but have they made great captains? Our best leaders have been tremendous players – Benaud, Bradman, Ian Chappell and, perhaps, Taylor (in case I am accused of disrespect by Messrs Bradman or Chappell Major, the order is strictly alphabetical). However, it is the captain who is a good player in his own right, and who is also aware of the personalities of each of the players in his team and the need for variation in thought, technique and philosophy, who will allow the team to bloom.

Under AB, Simpson enforced maleness in isolation, the aim being to reduce distraction and perhaps make life less embarrassing for the single men, especially on tour. I gained the impression from

Taylor's leadership that McGrath felt he could let it all hang out. The boy from Narromine felt much more secure with the captain from Wagga Wagga. At the same time, the lad from Launceston, the Good Bloke Boon, began to feel he was from a different generation, a different world.

Certainly, John Buchanan, who coached Queensland to their first Shield triumph, began having family barbecues, with children as guests, not hors d'oeuvres. Under Jeff Thomson, who learnt much under the mateship programme of the Chappells, maleness was the Queensland philosophy, as you would expect. These may be coincidences, but I think Taylor was more of a Thinker than a Bloke. And I hadn't seen an Australian team as hot as his since Ian Chappell's. In any case, there is a fair chance that Chappell's reign of Blokedom was also laced with thought and commonsense. Being a Bloke doesn't necessarily exclude thought. Perhaps Blokes will be Blokes when they want to be, when it suits. Underneath it all, I'll bet Ian Chappell is a real Wuss.

Taylor has broken the mould in the Australian team. This new mould would appear to be rather flexible, to allow, even expect, alternative thinking. The priority remains, to take wickets and score runs, but not mindlessly or mechanically. It has to be healthy for the game that our Test players are encouraged to develop their own styles in a creative, artistic sense while their own identities grow and are established through their personal endeavours.

A comparison with the West Indies seems instructive. Under Clive Lloyd, the team was full of self-confident people who were happy, relaxed and well-established. With Viv Richards' guidance, this allowed black politics, through Rastafarianism, to develop. While the outcome of Viv's politics wasn't particularly successful, it had existed in the team for a long time and was certainly a noticeable feature of the persona of Lloyd's successor.

Malcolm Marshall was his own, fiercely strong, man. Joel Garner could hardly be anything else but an individual. Similarly, there could only ever be one Michael Holding. Gordon Greenidge snapped and snarled and muttered and growled – to himself. In private, a very quiet, likeable man. Jeff Dujon was more vivacious, warmer. Quite happy to talk at any time, in the style of any international

Slater is an

Reiffel and

aren't in the

as Rod and

terms of

Was Boonie

feel

enthusiast.
McGrath
same league
Doug in
blokedom.
starting to
isolated?

philanthropist. Desmond Haynes was more excitable, affected more in the short term by the pervading mood and therefore prone to be less of a distinct, developed character. A great player nonetheless, and a terrific supporter of the team. Dessie was a founding member of that team; not until he was excluded did Richie Richardson's new-look side finally lose at home. To Taylor's developing outfit.

The rise of Caribbean cricket in the late Seventies, and its subsequent unprecedented dominance, relied to a great extent on the character and nature of Lloyd himself. I have never seen anyone play like Clive. I have never even seen an imitator. Nobody could get near him. He was a big man, very relaxed, moving with grace and ease, strong and quick. Most of all, Clive was Cool. At all times he seemed contented with life, and soberly, inwardly happy, exuding the glow of the self-assured.

When NSW defeated the West Indies at the SCG in 1984-85, when Lloyd and his comrades were at their peak, Clive was playing, but not as captain. At the end of the match, the teams met for a chat and he greeted me warmly, saying, "well done skipper". It was a genuine statement of congratulations from a man who was well aware of his own team's achievements yet was neither avaricious nor excessively proud. It was a flicker in time, yet I remember it well. It was a feeling I retain, that I associate with a purity of emotion – when the Blues were up there, however fleetingly, with the world's best. The West Indies were powerful and proud, but not too proud to see and understand what was occurring outside their intimidating dressing-room door.

For a long time, the Australian team seemed to need externally-imposed togetherness. Everyone rigorously performed the same repetitive training routine. Afterwards, they all played golf together. Wives and girlfriends were excluded from their everyday lives, although recreational visitation was a recognised off-duty prerogative. Alternative personalities were allowed if they performed strongly, people like Greg Matthews, Mike Whitney and Merv Hughes, but it seemed that any slip-up in their performance and the more malleable personalities became ready replacements. Understandably, it is easier to work with those who automatically follow your philosophy.

Since AB was only learning captaincy when he took over, there was no friction between him and Simpson. He could concentrate on his batting and the coach could teach him his philosophies and tactics. It was a successful partnership. Border's team remains the only one to win the World Cup for Australia. They were successful at home against all bar the West Indies, and they came pretty close to beating them. They annihilated England twice on their own pitches.

Eventually, the stern routine of imposed togetherness, which allowed coach and captain to comfortably go about their business, yielded established players like Taylor, Slater, Boon, Jones, Marsh, Hughes, McDermott and the Waughs. The side had the nucleus of self-confidence and the foundation on which to take the next small step – to real strength. Border saw the time was right to go. He was still a Test batsman, but his team had never quite reached the summit; under him, I don't think the team was ever going to take that next step. Perhaps, in time, he would have kept developing, but he played his part in the process and achieved a unique, magnificent record. Cricket does imitate life and art. Nobody's perfect.

Under Taylor, it seemed, there was more than just an expectation of performance. Undeniably, his team expected itself to perform, but it also had a thorough enjoyment of creative difference, learning and developing new techniques. Under Border, Warne became a bowler who won Tests through individual brilliance. Under Taylor, the team has not needed Warne, as its other components gelled so well that his fractured toe – and subsequent hand and shoulder ailments – did not seriously weaken their ability to bowl out the opposition. It was not that Warne was no longer a great bowler. Taylor knew only too well his strengths, abilities and tactics. It was just that the side reminded me of a strong Blues outfit, where everyone was encouraged to be good at everything, and not be satisfied.

At the same time, Slater's brilliant run as a batsman of daring impetuosity began to come to a halt. It appeared that he began to see the possibilities of failure through "bad shots" or "rashness", accusations that commentators throw at batsmen who don't quite manage to execute the courageous. People suggested to Slater that he was too aggressive. Every run scored involves risk. You might trip over and fall flat on your face cruising through for the single to fine leg. A batsman can never be too aggressive. Indeed, a batsman who needs a Test cricketer's income to service a half-million dollar mortgage on an excessively expensive $A800,000 Bondi residence, might be tempted to think he should stick to the positive approach that brought him those tangible rewards.

The deplorable irony of batting is that once you think you should be aggressive, that instinctive aggression is tempered. Batsmen who do best are those who are relaxed, focussed and not distracted by thought. Slater needed to forget about being positive, forget about his mortgage, and trust his instinct. He needed to develop the ability to clear his head, as his opening partner from Wagga Wagga had done. Doesn't it remind you of Luke Skywalker being taught how to fight Darth Vader? "Close your eyes and trust your instincts Michael. Be yourself. Believe. Believe." Easier said than done.

Mark Waugh is the gambler. He wins, he loses, he shrugs. But he remains unforceful, unaggressively feminine in his demeanour. Taylor called him "Pretty" for good reason. Mark survived the imposed male bonding, by scoring runs. He was not One Of The Boys: he was One Of A Kind. I suspect that early criticism of his back-away-and-cut style really annoyed some West Indies players, and probably Viv Richards more than most, because he was beating them at their own game. Mark played and enjoyed, just as it should be.

TAYLOR'S TEAM still had that hard-edged maleness. McGrath no longer cowered after a bad ball, hand running through his hair. He decided, on his own, that the time was right for him to bowl round the wicket: he felt no need to consult anyone. He would try the bouncer, and again. His sense of self had developed: now he was Glenn McGrath, Australian Bowler, Winner of Test Matches. The toughness of his upbringing in the bush would increasingly start to emerge as he destroyed opponents with increasing ruthlessness. It was his personality that would dismiss batsmen. He had little to think about but the thrill of taking wickets and the frustration of trying to learn to be a batsman.

No longer a stopgap, Paul Reiffel, too, emerged under Taylor. Slowly, the media began to view him as more than a fairly innocuous

Shield bowler. Personally, I can recall him being deadly on a ridge at St Kilda's Junction Oval as long ago as 1989. Half a decade later, under Taylor, he bowled out the Windies. And Pakistan. And Warne's injuries, remember, prevented him from taking more than a spasmodic role in those series, He was the quiet cornerstone of unexciting domination. I go to matches to watch good teams play well, more than to see tense finishes.

After the series was won in the Caribbean, there was great merriment to be had watching who attached themselves publicy to victory. The most entertaining piece of writing I have read in a long time was an article by Simpson in the *Sydney Morning Herald*. It produced a rare kaleidoscope of emotional responses from readers. At first glance, it seemed to be a clever, celebratory parody from the mind of some miscreant journalist who was awash with nationalistic, homesick joy. Statements ranged from "When I began coaching this time I was astounded at how little the players knew" all the way to: "They were a group of individuals who all looked after themselves and didn't care for the team or their team-mates. I had to restore pride in wearing the Australian cap, and re-establish the peer support network that existed when I first played in the team. I even had to teach the players how to field properly."

Steve Waugh was reported as saying that the Blokes looked after themselves when he came into the team, that they always seemed worried about keeping their places, which directly supported Simpson's points. The most obvious assumption is that following World Series Cricket, Australian players had become obsessed with money, greed and selfishness. Yet while this is the most obvious, it is also the most superficial assessment.

In my experience, the Test team desperately wanted to play well as A Team, primarily, perhaps, because cricket is a game of power struggles and no individual wants to play in a fragmented or weak team and be bombarded by the opposition, the media, their captain, their family or friends, with criticism or simpering, understanding, sympathetic irritations. The simple truth was that, pre-Simpson, the team was not a good one because it had many inexperienced players led by an inexperienced captain. Money, selfishness or the breakdown of history and tradition had little or no direct influence on those desperately tense players.

Despite Simpson's amazing revelations of self-worth, it is true that he alone had a profound effect on the team. He professed it to have been in the coaching of technique. Closer to the truth is the idea that there was a leadership vacuum that he filled off the field. He was able to develop self-confidence through those repetitious fielding sessions: they gave the players a wider, extroverted view of themselves as a team. Athleticism, even arrogance, could be celebrated. Players habitually performed the skills that would help dismiss the opposition, without mechanical preoccupation. However, it was the development of self-assurance and relaxation that allowed the likes of Hughes and Dean Jones to progress. Even AB began to unwind a little and reveal his true nature, at least in the better times.

All the same, there were players who were less cautious and overstepped the mark – according to Simpson; players, perhaps, such as Greg Dyer, Greg Ritchie, Wayne Phillips, Gilbert and Matthews, who allowed their personalities to be revealed carelessly. This flaunting was perceived as a direct threat to both Simpson – whose method of man-management involved dividing the plebs and ensuring loyalty to himself – and to the hidden persona of AB himself.

IRONICALLY, Taylor's rise to the captaincy meant that Simpson's role had become less valuable. Simpson's stated aim, at the commencement of his career, had rung true: his martyr-like predictions that the team would not need a coach had become a worryingly realistic prophecy. When that amazing article was written Simpson had moved into self-preservation mode. Hence the need to tell the world why he was such a great coach. The sad part of this was that it didn't need to be stated. He was the coach of an undermanned team which against all odds had defeated the world's best on their own turf for the first time in 23 years. His self-evaluation focused on happenings a decade earlier. It was egotistical, an embarrassing attempt to grab some of the spotlight. The coach's role is to assist the team, not to smuggle away stolen accolades that belong to the unit.

Taylor's captaincy quickly revealed cracks, perhaps developing wider chasms with every moment under Simpson's increasingly intense grasp of his position. Taylor appeared to have already taken the plunge, by dreaming of a proud, traditional Australian team, brimming with invincible self-belief. He was seeking the next level, searching deep for the inspiration to establish this wonder vision. He appeared, temporarily, to be struggling to tread water. A visit to the Murrumbidgee River in Wagga Wagga may have soothed his soul, taken him back to his in-utero place of spiritual birth. I can imagine him sitting against a gnarled willow tree, green hair cascading around his forehead, easing the conflict of opposing minds and voices that surrounded the team.

The water swirls and eddies, trickling and tinkling its glistening path, past that moment when Mark sits and drinks deeply. He might well have decided to slip into the muddied current, hidden from the public gaze, beneath the will of the people and beyond their clasping hands and minds. Such was the decision he had to make, having seen his vision of the team's future. He had looked in the dressing-room mirror, and seen over his shoulder the glances of men seeking strength, guidance, hope and a future. He had fallen in and swum for his life, taking others with him.

AB could have remained captain and achieved his aims. He began to believe that more could be achieved. He dipped in his toe and found the water not to his liking. It affected his batting and made him less brave, less able to ignore all others. The water made him look around and be distracted by the shouts of teammates. He chose to stay dry. He was scared of the current and he escaped unhurt. He had survived for so long on the banks of the Brisbane River. When he had scored more Test runs than Bradman what else was there to achieve as a batsman? Even the most meticulous, professional batsman can only mindlessly achieve upcoming milestones for so long before aimlessness sets in.

A CAPTAIN HAS a very narrow ledge on which to walk. He must be well-liked and respected. He must also manipulate his players' mental states and control their general thinking. He holds the power to cut a player's income, drastically. In the Test team, he can control a player's identity, ego and focus of endeavour. The captain who plays all these roles successfully is held in great reverence. He is feared, he is suspected; he is trusted and distrusted; he is the focus of admiration and loyalty. In a paternalistic system like cricket, if the physiotherapist is mother, the captain must be the father.

One of a father's most useful roles is to tell his children a story. This greatly aids their bonding as a family, their imaginations and education. It is part of the development of family tradition, passing down oral history to the next generation. At the very least, a good storyteller will be a well-loved father, with whom children love to spend their time. In Taylor's case, his self-confidence as a batsman also greatly assisted him to gain the respect of his boys, as though he were introducing children to Nintendo. The story of Australian cricket that Allan Border told him included the historic and subliminal chant of David Boon, high among the fast bowlers at table top, Huon Pine legs revealed in hairy, gnarled glory below his creamy, ACB knit mini skirt, socks on feet, embeered, teammates waiting to recite the solemn oath of brotherhood, Under the Southern Cross.

THE DIRECT EXPRESSION, "You fucking beauty", is an aggressive, basic, procreative attitude designed to assist the survival of the fittest. Maleness seeks fucking a beauty, a quick and explosive act, linked to physical appearance. It is a colloquial expression of maleness, but it can be seen to exclude femininity, and nurturing and supportive relationships. Border's reliance on strong, decisive, male, independent players is symbolic of "fucking", and the absence of collective psychology. Paradoxically, fucking can also be a group, sharing arrangement, of mateship. Cricket has this paradox.

The song's exclusion of women, or at least its attitude to them, was reflected in Border's exclusion of wives and girlfriends from the team hotel, so that the boys could be together. Yet ironically, his greatest advisor was his wife Jane, whose analytical understanding of the game, and her husband's mentality, allowed her great influence.

I can't imagine Taylor excluding women to the same extent. How could the Father of the Year, the man who shared the spotlight with his son at a post-Ashes Test press conference, exclude women? Certainly, by growing up – in cricket terms – in the NSW team, he will have learnt to celebrate diversity, and alternative thought and methodology. This has been a feature of the Blues' tactics in the Eighties and Nineties. Whitney, Matthews, the Waughs, Big Hen (Geoff Lawson), Dutchy (Bob Holland), Max (Murray Bennett) and Lizard (Dave Gilbert), to name but a few, were never the same, mould-fitting Blokes. Imran Khan taught us tricks and culture from Pakistan. The Blues taught Imran team unity that celebrated diversity. The Blues haven't been Good Blokes for a long time. ◐

Adapted from 'O My Captain' by Dirk Wellham

TED DEXTER & FRED TRUEMAN
HEADINGLEY, JUNE 1989

Mark Ray Three Lions and a Tiger

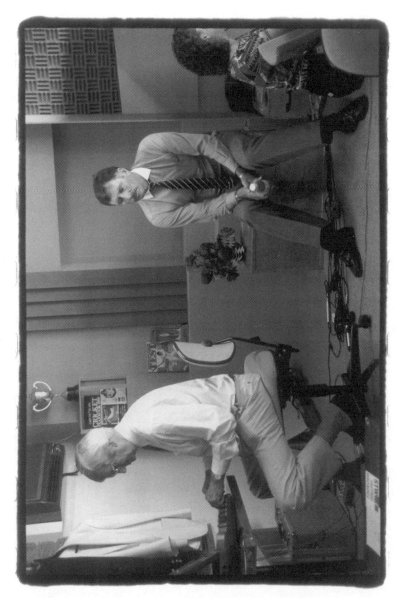

RICHIE BENAUD & IAN CHAPPELL CHANNEL NINE COMMENTARY BOX, PERTH, FEBRUARY 1991

Murray Hedgcock

Failing the Tebbit Test

Murray Hedgcock was born
in Melbourne, entered newspapers
in 1949, and worked in London
from 1953-55. Posted to the
London bureau of News Limited
of Australia in 1966, he has
written on cricket for *The
Australian* and other publications
– and is proud to hold both
Australian and UK citizenship.

Favourite Ashes innings
The innings I wish I had seen
is English (shame!) – Jessop's
75-minute century setting up the
one-wicket victory in the 1902
Oval Test.

**English cricket is less than
brilliant because...** in this
soccer-obsessed country, the best
athletic talent is creamed off into
that game, and cricket starves.

It is with much pride that I fail the Tebbit Test, despite having lived precisely half my life in London, and loving this country deeply – for all its oddities and faults.

I defend Britain against critics, and I find much to admire about the English. But when it comes to the indulgence that is sport, then I am firmly anti-English – a believer in the doctrine espoused by the radical Labour MP Dennis Skinner, "Anyone But England". I barrack against England in any sporting contest, for the simplest of reasons – I am by birth, background and upbringing an Australian from the era when the greatest of all sporting contests was the Ashes, and no genuine Australian could ever see England as anything other than The Enemy.

When England played that lesser 11-a-side game in the World Cup, I was at various times a fervent Tunisian, a loyal Romanian, a patriotic Colombian, and a reluctant but determined Argentinian. Quite apart from the basic belief that I could never support England in any sporting contest, there was always the fun of going against the popular stream – and the pleasure of monitoring Fleet Street and television's more raucous commentators bemoaning the results. Yes, *schadenfreude*, I admit – but what joy! And there is the fringe benefit that I know in the finish, I am just about bound to win at such times: the poor England supporter has only one chance for victory, as he sticks with his team inspired by St.George, but I get multiple chances as I move painlessly from one adopted loyalty to another.

The New Ball

My approach to sporting allegiance is much simpler and more agreeable when it comes to cricket; I quite enjoyed being a South African for much of the recent season, and then flying the flag for Sri Lanka. Zimbabwe success when their chicken-farmers and big-game hunters nailed that moaning bunch of English "professionals" in 1997 was a bonus: we Zimbabweans may be few in number, but we showed up the old colonial overlords! My policy is suspect only when it comes to the West Indies: I long detested their intimidatory bowling, which takes essential light and shade, grace and humour out of the game. But I grit my teeth, avert my eyes, lie back and think of being agin' England, rather than being for their opponents. It hurts a bit, but it's the only way out.

I came to England first in 1953: it was Coronation Year, but that was not the lure. I wanted to see Lindsay Hassett's team in action, fulfilling an Ashes dream of a decade. Cricket did not seduce me at an impossibly youthful age: light dawned when I was nine, after my father bought me *The Game of Cricket as it Should be Played*, in the One Shilling Foulsham's Sports Library. It was 1941: I played cricket in the barely-organised fashion of a primary school of 100 pupils in a Victorian country town of fewer than a thousand people. Here was a new if distant world: who, I wondered, were Messrs Hobbs, Tate and Strudwick, who helpfully explained how I could play this fascinating game? They were English, true, but that was acceptable: England was where the game had originated, and so we Aussies acknowledged their quality.

Mr Hobbs wore a risibly long sweater in some of the photographs: it was ironic that 20-odd years later, I was to play two seasons of club cricket in England without needing any such item of clothing – and then having to buy one on return to Australia, to play at Mildura, in Victoria's burning Mallee. The photographs also included eight pictures of "Famous 'Test' Australians": Macartney and Gregory, Taylor and Collins, Oldfield and Mailey, Bardsley and Ryder. They didn't mean much to me: where was the one and only Bradman? (I later found the book had been published in 1926, the year before The Don made his first-class debut). Cricket soon became a factor added to life from a much loftier direction than a mere book. Moved to the Dandenong Ranges, just outside Melbourne, I went to school at Upwey, and one day my parents told me a new headmaster had been appointed who was quite famous. "Have you heard of Bill Woodfull?" they asked. I blush to reveal that I had not, but it turned out he had been Australia's Test captain – senior even to Don Bradman. For years I have, if not quite dined out on being a pupil of WM Woodfull, then dropped the news into conversation, usually on the angle that I have a multiple collection of cricket autographs – those Woodfull signatures in my school report book. (Most confirm form teachers' comments such as, "Murray does the minimum required of him", or "Murray would achieve a happier school life if he co-operated more" – but that is another matter). To our disappointment, Upwey High School life did not become cricket-dominated, or even orientated: Bill Woodfull, son of a Methodist minister, was a dedicated schoolmaster who had rejected a knighthood, offered for his services to cricket, on the honourable grounds that this was only a game, and any award should be for his career in education. So cricket was no more than a modest sub-section of life: we who studied under him were asked to work hard, and reserve sporting interest for sporting sessions only. But there was a glimpse of the world Woodfull had once inhabited, when a school exhibition was staged, to which teachers and pupils were invited to bring objects of interest. The Head contributed – and I remember them well, half a century on – a signed photograph of King George V, and a letter from Sir James Barrie. These were the fruits of Test cricket – mementoes of great significance from men of great importance. What must it be like to play cricket for Australia – and to tour England, wearing the Baggy Green Cap?

It was not long before I realised that dreams of wearing That Cap would remain just dreams – but one day, perhaps, I could go to England, and watch Test cricket there. World War Two still raged, but of all the benefits of peace to anticipate, the resumption of Ashes cricket was one of the most appealing. I had been seven when the last series had been played, too young to know or care; now moving into my teens, the vision was very special. Cricket awareness was still limited: I was never – shameful to confess – one of those aficionados who sat up till 3.30 a.m. in a dark room, crouched over the receiver, to listen through the atmospherics to the progress of their team across the seas. The reason is simple: I was never able to stay awake, and usually gave up when lunch was taken, providing an immediate incentive to sleep.

But I still have a half-completed scrapbook on that magical first tour of 1948, one of the few teams whose names I can rattle off, beginning with The Don, and going down to the chaps who sang "the groundstaff bowlers' song", on the basis that they were rarely wanted in matches – Colin McCool and Doug Ring. That was the tour and the year that rekindled the fire of ambition: one day I would go to England and watch an Australian team in action. And I would go to barrack fervently for my country, and oppose the England team, like any genuine Aussie.

The right and proper attitude between our countries was spelled out in *Wisden* for 1972, when Ted Dexter wrote a "Welcome Australia" feature, beginning with the blunt statement of belief: "I have on occasions taken a quite unreasonable dislike to Australians... Given suitable circumstances... there can be few so absolutely right for a spot of disliking than a Test match between us Pommies and our most respected cricketing foes... Under provocation no greater than is needed to stimulate our own aggression, Australians can, and do... throw off all their 180 years of civilised nationhood; they gaily revive every prejudice they ever knew, whether to do with accent, class-consciousness or even the original convict complex, and sally forth into battle with a dedication which would not disgrace the most committed political agitators."

This is splendid knockabout stuff, even if it overlays with a somewhat flippant approach a genuine feeling between our worlds which Dexter went on to explain with absolute logic:

"The indisputable fact is that we come from the same stock, and can therefore indulge ourselves rather splendidly in an orgy of superficial hate, which our consciences cannot possibly allow in relation to any of the other cricketing nations with whom we consort." When in 1989 Dexter became the chairman of the new England Committee, charged not just with Test team selection, but also a range of associated duties, I had much pleasure at the subsequent press conference, in asking – with my best Aussie accent, just to get the point across – if Dexter recalled that declaration of nearly two decades earlier, and whether he still felt the same?

Shame on him: the new chairman smiled, almost embarrassed, made some feeble riposte to the effect, "Did I really say that?", and wandered into politician-speak, to indicate that no such forthright comments would come from his newly-diplomatic lips ever again. It was maddening on two counts. First, I had been deprived as a journalist of a nice story ("I still hate Aussies, says new England supremo Lord Ted") and secondly, the man representing English cricket had retreated from what to me was a right and proper stance of continuing hostility between our two cricketing worlds.

THIS ANTAGONISM is a cricket matter only (and of course a good-humoured one), not least for someone like myself who has shared his life between England and his native land. There is an ambivalence about living here so long, and setting roots so deep into English life, not least when I am just third-generation Australian: my family comes from Kent on my father's side, Cornwall on my mother's, and there could be nothing more truly symbolic of this country than such origins.

Raucous Australian criticism of "the Poms" annoys me intensely, partly because it is not in my nature to be raucous – and certainly not at cricket. And anyone slating English cricket, for all its oddities and imperfections, sparks my reflex wish to defend it, or at least content myself with the unexpressed thought: "Yes, mate – you wouldn't understand, because our country is still a new country, with none of the deep-seated traditions, and therefore inherent contradictions and weaknesses, that have long been built into this world of Pommies." So when a newly-arrived newspaper colleague was my guest for his first visit to Lord's, I was miffed by his amusement at the slope of the ground, the antiquated scoreboard, and the umpires in ankle-length coats (before they adopted Australian-style jackets which had led English writers to claim our umpires looked like stop-me-and-buy-one ice-cream sellers). That colleague and I have kept up a running battle over the years, as he has become more internationally-minded, wrapped in the sub-continent, and arguing that cricket must acknowledge the significance of the game there, discarding the mystique shrouding

Ashes cricket. I take the opposite view, maintaining that ultimate cricket is indeed Ashes cricket, and all else simply takes its place at the foot of the pedestal. The internationalist is Michael Coward, special writer on cricket for *The Australian* – the country's national daily – who loves his London and England, but does not let a generally romantic nature soften his bleak vision of Ashes cricket. In the run-up to the 1997 Australian tour of England, Mike responded bitterly after coach Geoff Marsh said it was a problem every four years to get the best out of Australian players: "Every cricketer dreams of going to England, and that is the pressure every player is putting on themselves".

Mike lashed out in fierce reply: "English cricket is an irrelevance. No doubt this year's tour will provide the Australian players with a pleasurable and memorable experience, but it will not provide them with a robust challenge. What it does provide is a handsome retainer for four months' work; a priceless entry in the Ashes history books; a possible sighting or an introduction to Mick Jagger and Paul Getty; assured success on the ground and a good time off it, provided a sober and aware management can keep the notorious (Fleet Street) tabloids at bay... Is it any wonder that anyone worth his bat, ball and box will bust a gut to get abroad the gravy train?"

Matthew Engel reported this in *The Guardian* as an indication of the low esteem in which English cricket was held, also recording Coward's wish to see Australia win Tests in Asia – "cricket's new world, the real world". Engel added thoughtfully: "He remains in a minority. Most Australians still want to keep bashing England."

That is probably the case – but it also points up a modern problem for Australian cricket: Australians these days will go to see their team bash England for first preference, or anyone else, but if the wheel turns and it is the home team which gets bashed, then Australian interest, as measured by crowds, disappears like a shower on a hot day at the MCG. The media too turns away, and cricket is relegated well inside the sports section, just edging out the softball, lacrosse, and perhaps the soccer reports from wintry England.

Mike Coward is not alone in his scorn for current Ashes confrontation. When the 1997 Australians came to England, Malcolm Conn, cricket correspondent of *The Australian*, wrote a

Australia collapsed; I **suffered** in silence. Brown hit Jarman. Big bully. Coming from Adelaide, I felt **protective** scornful pre-tour study declaring it was "difficult to understand why England is still so widely regarded as a champagne series. Playing the beleaguered Poms is cheap and unfulfilling. There is little challenge and hollow joy in beating an opponent who has forfeited all right to play in the same division... Seventeen Australian cricketers fortunate enough to spend the Northern summer feasting on what should be relatively easy pickings had better make every ray of sunshine count."

Mal being a mate, I felt slightly embarrassed at informing Fleet Street of his opinions, but it seemed the sort of attitude that was increasingly held in Australia, and best that the locals know about it. And I was stirred to the point of preparing the following declaration, which was displayed at my second Test spot in the Lord's press box:

STATEMENT OF INTENT
This desk is barracking for England – as a matter of cricketing principle, in protest at the belief widely held in Godzone (country) that:
a) The Tour would be an Australian picnic,
and
b) The Ashes no longer matter much.
A policy review may be made later in the series.

In the finish I returned to instinct and barracked for Australia in the rest of the series, because by then England had got a bit cocky, and of course I disapproved of the Melbourne-born, Ballarat-encouraged Hollioakes playing against the land of their birth.

Incidentally the Cowards and Conns are not the first to see little point in playing England. Remember a chap called Frank Allan, "The Bowler of a Century"? He was an outstanding left-arm medium-pace bowler for Victoria, who would have been picked in the first Test of all, at the MCG in March 1877, except for his stated preference to visit the Warrnambool Show and meet his friends there. Warrnambool is one of my several home towns, and I have played cricket on those Showgrounds – but I do feel Frank Allan was missing something. You may know that picture of the 1878 Australian team in England; Allan is the chap second from left in the front row, looking a bit sheepish, practically skulking in fact. Had he by then realised just what he had denied himself a year earlier? I think we should be told...

But my loyalty to my Australia is not blind and automatic. Loyalty is a two-way business – and when in 1982 the South African-born, English county-educated Kepler Wessels was picked for Australia, I used my sports column in *The Australian* to declare my dismay at what I saw as my country's desertion of national principle. How *Could* they pick a travelling mercenary, calculatedly making a living from cricket in not even his second, but his third country? Yes, he had settled there, he had an Australian wife – but did this make him Australian? Certainly not in cricketing terms, whatever the citizenship or residential qualification. Suddenly I wanted this pseudo-Australia to lose when it included Wessels, because it was not my Australia, not real Australia, no longer dinkum.

Kerry Packer had hijacked Australian cricket, imposing his wishes for its presentation and promotion, to the point that I lost all enthusiasm for the team and the cause that had for 30-odd years been central to my cricketing enjoyment and motivation. But the great glory of cricket is that its principles always win out in the end, and by 1989, after more change, I felt able to declare in another column that I had rejoined the colours, because I believed the new Australia was again the true Australia.

My sports editor, grabbing a chance to stir the possums, gave this column unusual display in *The Australian*, under the line, "Murray Hedgcock despises Australia's TV-dominated cricket era of limited overs but all is forgiven now – Hey boys, I'm back on board". I scanned with much embarrassment this slice of big-noting: who on earth would care what I felt? Would anyone even read it? Yes – a few days later came a personal note from the chairman of the Australian Cricket Board, to say simply: "Welcome back". I felt relieved – and justified.

But if my loyalty was tested beyond breaking point by the Wessels affair, before being repaired by events, then my opposition to England has been strengthened by indignation ever since 1972 when that country, desperate for an all-rounder, decided Tony Greig was qualified. No matter that he spent seven months of each year in his native South Africa: he played for Sussex during the brief English summer – and hey presto, he was English. I was bitter at this chicanery, and wrote a column seeking to drum up opposition to Greig's inclusion. But no-one in Australia seemed bothered, England certainly was not going to take note, and so Greig became English – until five years later he led the Packer revolt. Then the respected John Woodcock received quite unjustified stick for writing in *The Times* that Greig was an Englishman "not by birth or upbringing, but only by adoption. It is not the same thing as being English through and through". Of course Woodcock was right. I have spent vastly more time in England than ever did Tony Greig; my family links are genuine English – but I don't consider myself English, and I am very different in upbringing, attitude and feeling to the genuine home product. What's more, I wouldn't want to play cricket for England, in the improbable event of my residential qualification leading to such an invitation; it simply would not seem right.

I still cannot really understand how any true Englishman could unquestioningly accept Greig and Lamb, Chris and Robin Smith, McCague and Mullally, Gallian and Caddick, and then the Hollioakes. English cricket certainly accepted them, clutched at them, in hope of strengthening the Test team – and who cared where its players came from? Worst of all was the speeded qualification for Graeme Hick, an act of appalling opportunism – on a par with the way the runner Zola Budd gained UK citizenship in record time, to compete for Britain in the Olympics. How *could* they be so unpatriotic as to trawl the world – or so it seemed – for recruits? Was this the meaning of Empire?

And on reflection, I believe this is the answer. For centuries the British Empire was built on the products, services and people discovered abroad and brought back to strengthen the Mother Country. It became an accepted basis of operation – and so in sport, the same principle applied long after Empire was gone, and the world coloured pink on the school atlas was reduced in effect to the United Kingdom. And it's no new development; I was startled on reading association football history, to learn how back in the 1880s, top English clubs would recruit Scots professionals – no matter that a

Scot had nothing at all to do with Burnley or Arsenal, Wolves or Aston Villa. From the Sixties onwards, county cricket operated on much the same pattern, but hiring overseas players – which in 1972 brought the bizarre spectacle of Warwickshire winning the championship with four West Indian Test players. Good Brummies? Very funny. The only dissenting note then, as now, was concern that outsiders deprived local talent of opportunity, while giving the temporary residents experience that in time would be used against their host country. This has never seemed to me to be the point: the key issue is that these aliens are there at all, freely given their false colours, when they should be learning their craft in their own land, and strengthening its domestic game – not confusing the make-up of English teams. Nowhere do I feel this more deeply than with Hick: he should have been for a decade putting polish and punch into Zimbabwe, to help its Test progress – not masquerade as English. Hence, I tend to adjust the prayer of the youthful Cardus: "Please God, let Australia be all out for 120 – Trumper 100". I appeal: "Let England be all out for 120 – and Hick get a first-ball duck."

So I barrack for Australia as truly representing my country – while an England Xl does not truly represent England. It's as simple as that. My workable definition of qualification, given the mobility of society today, would be that you play for the country where you learned your cricket – which would cut out most of the foreign-born or educated players brought into recent England sides. And please don't niggle that Plum Warner was born in the Caribbean, Jardine and Cowdrey in India, Dexter in Italy, Gubby Allen in Australia: they were simply following the middle-class lifestyle of their day, and they were still truly English in the way they lived, studied, worked and played.

So there was further reason to object to and barrack against England's Test team: it was not truly English, whereas my Australia – except for that dreadful Wessels lapse – was indeed The Real Thing. I accept that the purist might argue, "In that case, where are the aborigines in Australian Test sides?" – and he has a point. It is a shadow on our cricket that the talents of the original people have not been encouraged to Test level – although ironically aborigines have played for the Australian women's national team. I accompanied the 1988 Aboriginal party, managed by that great fly-half Mark Ella, for much of its tour of England, when the stated aim was to get an aboriginal into the Test team within five years; sadly, none of the party made any further advance, and the initiative fizzled out.

Becoming an MCC member in 1971 – being proposed at a time when the waiting list was modest – was a true thrill for this outsider, because of the feeling I held for cricketing tradition. To join a club dating back before Australia was colonised represented a personal acceptance by history that gave me a real pride in belonging. For anyone luxuriating in the game's background as I had done for so long, MCC and Lord's represented institutionalised truth, the heart of cricket and all it meant. Yes, the aristos at Lord's in 1933 had got it wrong about Bodyline, but then, they were simply being true to their own caste and creed: now perhaps I even had the chance to inject a little Australian reality, a new perspective into this still-cloistered world.

That splendidly rebellious character Rowland Bowen – born into conventional middle-class Britain, but an uncomfortable part of it – once wrote scathingly of the Long Room suddenly full of provincial social-climbers, flaunting their ties and their membership of this once-exclusive club. "Like NCOs admitted to the officers' mess," he declared fiercely – with bizarre snobbery for such a radical. When I inquired whether a similar description applied to me as a newly-rejoicing member, Bowen was sporting/kind/tactful enough to say no, that was another matter: colonials had every right to join, and to enjoy their acceptance. (He had a great deal of time for Australia and Australians, despite the astonishing disparity between our world and his).

In my early days in London I was something of the token Aussie, the Fifties being just before hordes of tourists and working backpackers set out for England as part of their trip to the Old World. I remember being almost exhibited as an interesting specimen at a 1955 winter luncheon of The Cricket Society, held in the old Tavern while Lord's was under snow; my status gained me a seat next to the guest of honour, Jim Laker. Big Jim should have been in Australia with Hutton's team, as the loyal assembly unanimously declared: I felt strange, isolated, because their wish for triumph in distant

Australia was absolutely opposed to my loyalties – and yet it was more important that we were all cricket lovers, regardless of partiality, and here were a couple of hours to savour for that binding interest, England and Australia together.

But you always get back to confrontation, and rightly so, in this glorious game. For years I have enjoyed a running correspondence with a Cheshire-based Yorkshireman named Roy Ramsbottom, who is conducting a one-man crusade to rehabilitate Douglas Jardine. The captain who won back the Ashes in 1932-33 has been sadly misunderstood and traduced even in English cricket, which benefited by his devotion to duty (Roy believes); I argue the point, and our non-stop debate is enormous fun. "The longest whinge in sporting history," the quirky Simon Barnes has called Australia's traditional complaint about Bodyline. Not really, Simon; we just feel we were deceived, because England had preached Corinthian values of sport as expressed at their highest level by cricket – and then as we raised our sights to the stars, Larwood and Co. hit us below the belt. Who did this bloke Jardine think he was – an Aussie? This argument will run and run...

So there is debate, and there is joy – and there is anguish. I don't think I have ever spent a more miserable day at cricket than at Lord's on Monday, June 24, 1968, when in a soup-like atmosphere, the grass practically sprouting as we watched, Australia collapsed for 78 in reply to England's weather-protracted seven for 351. Doug Walters made 26; John Gleeson, improbably, was the only other man in double figures, and David Brown and Barry Knight were world-beaters. I sat sullenly in the bottom tier of the old Nursery End Stand, gloomy and dank enough at the best of times, and felt all the woes of Northern weather pressing in on me as the crowd rejoiced at the fall of the invaders, and I suffered in silence. A 50-minute rain-break in mid-afternoon, and a similar stoppage after the teams were presented to the Queen at tea, just added to the general air of damp desolation.

This was not cricket. How on earth did they ever manage to invent the game in a country of such weather? Poor Barry Jarman had a chipped finger – and so Brown promptly hit him on the same finger with a kicker when he came in to bat. Big bully! Play the game, you

The New Ball

Pommy cad! Having come to England from Jarman's home town of Adelaide, I felt protective of the poor chap – while all those fiendish spectators howled for his blood, and more. It was little consolation to learn later that the Australians had celebrated with too much enthusiasm a birthday the previous evening – that of the cricket correspondent from my own newspaper. But it all came right in the end as our brave blokes hung on for a stubborn draw, with Ian Redpath, my South Melbourne hero (I always had a hero from the current South eleven), scoring a dogged half-century, and the elegant Paul Sheahan playing one of the most valuable scoreless innings in Test history. He stayed a full 50 minutes for his 0 not out – and English critics had the nerve to complain that the weather saved Australia, as only two and a half hours' play was possible on the final day. Given that Australia had suffered initially because of that same sort of weather – producing conditions to delight any seam bowler – this seemed to me a monstrous mis-reading (deliberate, of course) of the match. And another case history was there to support my policy of barracking against England teams at all times, in all sports.

It was much worse at The Oval two months later, when interfering busybodies from the crowd augmented the official groundstaff to drain a sodden ground, and allow a late passage of play which cost us the match, and a series victory. Remember? England won with five minutes to spare when John Inverarity was given lbw to Derek Underwood (I still maintain it was a crook decision) – and the pavilion rose as one man to acclaim home heroes. I was sitting on the top deck – and displaying great restraint and presence of mind, I stifled a groan of agony, and leaped to my feet, to show solidarity with all around me. Well, not solidarity; just self-preservation, as it seemed one solitary sitting spectator, clearly not sharing the general rejoicing, might have been at risk of being hurled over the railing into the rushing crowds below. I trudged home a sore loser...

But for cricketing delight showered upon the deserving head of this expatriate, nothing could beat "Massie's Match", when on June 26, 1972, the West Australian Bob Massie completed the astonishing figures of 16 wickets for 137 on his Test debut. Two memories endure from my Long Room monitoring of the day: first, an ideal view of the extraordinary way in which Massie curved the ball (no need for abstruse theories about "reverse swing" and other technicalities beloved of latterday pundits); and then, the delighted but genuinely embarrassed expression on the face of amiable Bob as he clumped his way into the pavilion, applauded all the way by a defeated but generous crowd. And 20 years later, called in to give my amateur (rather than expert) radio comments when visiting a Sheffield Shield match in Perth, I found myself at the microphone alongside Massie – the first time I had met him. It was a minor scoop to tell Australian Broadcasting Corporation listeners that I had not seen this chap since the memorable day when He Blushed At Lord's...

You see, contrary to popular belief, we Australians are sensitive characters, responding with shy appreciation to a kind word. And if you English didn't see it that way when The Don carved up your attack, when Ian Chappell led the sledging, when Lillee and Thomson dropped the ball about your ears, when Shane Warne applied his own exquisite torture – well, maybe you shouldn't have dumped your spare convicts in Terra Australis, and then taught us how to play cricket. ◖

RECORDER OF HISTORY: DAVID FRITH LONGPARISH, HAMPSHIRE, JULY 1997

MAKERS OF HISTORY: THE BEDSERS AND WAUGHS ADELAIDE, JANAURY 1994

Gideon Haigh

Jack Iverson: Tragic Magic

Gideon Haigh, a pure Anglo-Australian (and proud of it), writes about business as a professional, cricket as an amateur. His books include *The Cricket War*, *One Summer Every Summer*, *The Border Years* and *The Summer Game*, winner of this year's Australian Cricket Society Literary Award. He has just completed a history of the investment bank BT Australia. His favourite shot is the back-foot defensive.

Favourite Ashes innings
As an obstinate schoolboy opener, I was nicknamed Tavaré, so when Chris broke his bonds at Melbourne in 1982 to score a stylish 89, mine was the loudest voice in the Ponsford Stand. Is anyone in the market for a biography, *Chris Tavaré: Tormented Genius of Cricket*?

England are so crap because... I suspect this question is one of the reasons. The capacity for self-flagellation appears limitless. The national team has the talent and resources to run Australia close. It should stop apologising for itself.

At 2.35pm on 23 October 1973, Victorian Police Constable Esmond O'Reilly attended on a Melbourne address after an apparent shooting fatality. In a 30 x 12 foot shed at the rear of the double-fronted Victorian home, he found a man lying with the muzzle of a .22 calibre rifle still on his chest, blood round his face and mouth.

Nothing distinguished it from a routine suicide investigation, other than that the fingers still in the trigger mechanism had for one crowded hour almost a quarter of a century before been the most talked about in cricket. With them, Jack Iverson had created a sub-genre of spin bowling with a membership of one and tilted an Ashes series Australia's way.

The news came as a shock to erstwhile colleagues. A few years ago, I was seated at lunch alongside Bill Brown when Iverson's name came up in conversation. The charming and personable Queenslander, who was his first Australian captain, was still perplexed. "Why would Jack do a thing like that?" he kept asking. "Do you know?" I couldn't advise him. Even David Frith, in his assiduous chronicle of cricketers' suicides *By His Own Hand*, concludes: "The nature of his death was not made public, and no-one outside the family seems able to point to a reason for the 58-year-old cricketer's action in the face of an apparently successful business and contented family life."

Yet, as Albert Camus once wrote of suicide: "An act like this is prepared within the silence of the heart, as is a great work of art." A quarter of a century after his death, I wondered, was there any chance of finding why Jack Iverson quit first cricket, then life, with such suddenness?

JUSTIFYING MY CURIOSITY was not difficult. In his own small way, Jack Iverson remains news. The property section of *The Age* newspaper of 8 August reported that his old Brighton home was to be sold. It described him as "the famous Test bowler with the unique leg-spin grip", and anyone curious could have found photographic verification in a dozen well-known cricket works.

There it is: the ball clasped snugly between the thumb and a folded middle finger like it's being given a Masonic handshake. Extending that middle finger while maintaining the fulcrum of the opposable thumb turned cricket physics on its head. From the same grip, with slight alterations of the hand's angle at release, Iverson bowled top-spinners and wrong 'uns that looked like leg-breaks, leg-breaks that resembled off-breaks. If spin bowling is the art of deceit, Iverson was up there with the Hitler diarists.

Iverson, however, is unique in other respects. Australian cricket abounds in comet-trail careers: about four in 10 players in its annals have played five Tests or fewer. Usually, however, it is because the unique demands of Test cricket stretch them beyond their talent and technique, or because form deserts them at inopportune moments, or because rivals of similar ability are in abundance.

That was not the case with Iverson. For five years from 1946, he was perhaps the world's most destructive bowler. In all classes of cricket, he took more than 400 wickets at a cost of less than 15. He headed the bowling averages in Brighton's premiership season of 1947-48, then in Melbourne's of 1948-49. He headed the Sheffield Shield averages and the first-class averages on an undefeated tour of New Zealand in 1949-50. And in 1950-51, the Test averages in a 4-1 Ashes victory.

For most who make the top level of cricket, moreover, it is the result of years of toil and aspiration. Not for Iverson. That crowded hour was virtually the sum of his cricket life: he was 31 when he took the game up, 37 when he played last for Victoria. And the ultimate struggle for Iverson, the one he could not win, was apparently the one within himself.

THE FIRST HALF of Iverson's life provides us with few clues. Second child and only son of estate agent Henry William Iverson and his wife Edith, John Brian Iverson was born in the Melbourne suburb of St Kilda on 27 July 1915.

At the age of nine, he was sent to board at Geelong College, a small but historic public school steeped in the English educational precept that young men should not only be able to recite their hic, haec, hocs but also execute a decent cover drive. In the school magazine, *Pegasus*, correspondents debated such subjects as "Is refinement effeminate?" and "Why communism would ruin Australia". They submitted such poems as *To The Commander of the R101 Who Stayed At His Position Among Flames Until the End*.

Here a boy could learn a lifetime alleigance to cricket. The grounds were picturesque and beautifully-maintained. Revered coach Percival Lloyd Williams ran nets five nights a week. Cynosure of all eyes was Lindsay Hassett, for five seasons a member of College First XI, as well as captain of football and tennis. One school song even borrowed from Newbolt to exhort:

Sons of the school who are there today
You must exalt her name
In study and on fields of play
Play up and play the game.

Jack Iverson, though, did not. There are vestigial traces of him in school records. In September 1927, for instance, he played the title role in an adaptation of The Mikado. In February 1929, as a medium-pace bowler, he captained the under-15 B-section paddock XI. He was awarded colours by his Morrison House, but never proceeded further than the school's 2nd XI, and the Valete for December 1933 mentions no honours either academic or sporting.

Harry Iverson next sent Jack jackarooing* in the Mallee – an informal finishing school for many young Australian males of the time – and he ended up as assistant manager at "Landscape": a 3,500-acre property on the Goulburn River owned by the eminent Australian industrialist Essington Lewis.

---

* Work of a roustabout or sheep station hand, for those unconversant with 'Strine

The New Ball

Iverson visited Maldon regularly, an old gold town proud of its association with Australian skipper Bill Woodfull. But when he went, it was to play golf: he won the club championship in 1935. And by the time 24-year-old Iverson enlisted in the Australian Imperial Force on 30 May 1940, he was beyond the age by which cricket has usually captivated.

"WAR," WROTE THE AMERICAN jurist Oliver Wendell Holmes, "is an organised bore." His experience was of the American Civil War, but his observation still held water a century later as Allied and Axis armies groped about in search of one another across the vast landscapes of Africa and the Pacific, brief and costly contacts interspersed with protracted periods of inactivity.

It was during these extended hibernations in hostilities, Iverson would say, that his method was born. Where B J T Bosanquet's "googly"/ "bosie" originated in a tennis-ball game called "twisti-twosti" at Oxford University, Iverson's prestidigitation was first rehearsed in ping-pong-ball and ruler games of French cricket while serving in New Guinea with the 2nd/4th Light Anti-Aircraft Regiment.

History does not record who were Bosanquet and Iverson's opponents at twisti-twosti and French cricket, which is a shame, for they are like the Mr Watsons to Alexander Graham Bells: coincidentally present at the creation of a profound innovation. We do know, thanks to Ray Robinson, that it was one Steve Henderson who was Iverson's captain in a unit match when the wannabe spinner first trialled his wiles. And when the first ball Iverson attempted with his grip disappeared for six into the kanai grass, Henderson retorted: "Cut out that nonsense, Jake – we've got enough runs to chase already."

That Iverson did not cut out that nonsense he ascribed to a chance meeting at Jolimont Park, which neighbours the Melbourne Cricket Ground. Having married Dorothy Jean de Tracy in July 1944 and been demobbed as a lance sergeant on 5 September 1945, Iverson ran across a match involving cricketers from the Melbourne School For the Blind. As R S Whitington narrated in *Sporting Life* in October 1950:

The courage and persevering determination of those blind players began a train of thought and resolve working in Iverson's mind. "If those chaps with all their handicap can do as well as that, I'm going to give my bowling discovery a go," muttered Jack, more to the nearest oak tree and the summer air than to his wife.

"And Johnny, if you take it up, I know you well enough to be certain you will finish in there," said Jean Iverson, pointing to the adjoining MCG.

The story of Iverson's epiphany, which Whitington described as "one of the sporting romances of the decade", has always seemed to me almost too exquisite to be true. But the cause is perhaps less important than the effect: in December 1946 Iverson found his way to the local Brighton club and was selected for its third XI. He must have seemed an unusual sight: a towering, craggy figure of 6ft 3in, his burly 15-stone physique squeezed into old flannels a couple of sizes too small, his massive, prehensile fingers coiled round the ball as though for an outsized game of marbles. But on his first day's cricket in 13 years, he took 15 Sandringham wickets for 25. Promoted to the first XI, he finished the season with 65 wickets.

Iverson was fortunate in his captain Dudley Fitzmaurice. A former South Melbourne and Victorian batsman, Fitzmaurice insisted that Iverson practice his bowling 10 hours a week. Iverson complied, strengthening his levering finger and cultivating the uncommon accuracy that would be his hallmark, and it paid dividends when his 79 wickets at 10 carried off the 1947-48 sub-district flag for his team.

When Iverson joined Melbourne in October 1948, his career trajectory became almost vertical. He claimed 64 wickets at an average of 12, including five for 59 in the final against South Melbourne won by 67 runs (the only man to resist long, ironically, was his schoolboy contemporary Hassett with 122). Capped by his state in November 1949, Iverson took 46 wickets at 16.6. Opposing batsmen were baffled, his home crowd bewitched. Queenslander Ken Mackay recalled the tumult when he became a victim: "I played confidently for a leg-break, but it zipped the other way and I was stranded down the wicket. How the Melbourne crowd loved it. Cushions and hats went flying in the air...Iverson was a wizard."

The New Ball

Taken to New Zealand in Bill Brown's second-string national squad in February 1950, Iverson then mowed down 75 wickets at 7.73. Less than four years after renouncing the ping-pong ball in favour of a cricket ball, Jack Iverson was about to become a full-fledged Australian cricketer.

WHAT MANNER OF CRICKETER was Jack Iverson? His cardinal virtue as a spinner, of course, was that he was virtually unintelligible from the hand.

There was actually a simple logic to his bowling – the ball turned whichever way his thumb pointed – but only the most eagle eye could detect it. Even his Melbourne and Victorian 'keeper Dr Ian McDonald had to rely on a more obvious signal: Iverson would swivel a different way at the end of his run according to which delivery he was bowling.

Iverson's variations were allied to precise, almost robotic, accuracy. Starting with hands together, as though to conceal his artifice, he approached the wicket diagonally with an economical seven-pace run. His action was a little open-chested, but he delivered from a full height and his body-swing and follow-through were exemplary.

Here was an outstanding bowler all right. Here was also, teammates found, an elusive character. For one, Iverson was uninterested in any aspect of cricket other than his bowling, even field placing. "Give me a silly mid-on, a silly-point and a keeper," he would tell his Melbourne skipper Jack Green. "You can do what you like with the rest." He was a negligible batsman – indeed, he did not own a bat until the club gave him a well-worn Edgar Mayne Specially Selected – and a clumsy liability in the field.

For another, Iverson was not one to join in cricket's social side. While most Victorian teammates spent their daily allowances on communal dinners at their lodgings, Iverson was known as the "spies and speas" man, ducking off on his own to streetside and railway station kiosks to ingest a staple diet of pie and peas.

There was also a sense that Iverson took fortune's blows harder than most. If someone took to his bowling at practice, he would shift unobtrusively to a neighbouring net. On the rare occasions in matches that batsmen made it difficult for him, Iverson would fret over whether his encryptions had been permanently decoded. Once against Fitzroy, he simply left the field, and would not return until Ian McDonald talked him round.

Melbourne teammate Clive Fairbairn remembers particularly the first time Iverson went wicketless for the club, how he joined his teammates in the showers disconsolately: "I've told you blokes all along I can't bowl. That proves it. I'm not playing again. I'm retiring."

Fairbairn's new-ball partner Jack Daniel could hardly believe his ears: "Aw, c'mon. Fairy and I get that sorta treatment every week. We don't complain about it. You're weak as buggery."

When the vow was left hanging, Fairbairn was deputised to get Iverson back for the next round against the powerful Collingwood. Over tea and a sandwich in Iverson's backyard, Fairbairn geed his teammate up. One bad week meant nothing. Iverson had the talent to succeed: there was no-one like him, perhaps anywhere. Eventually, he assented. OK, he'd play against Collingwood.

Collingwood's combative skipper Keith Stackpole Sr leered sadistically as he won the toss the following Saturday. The pitch was flat, the day warm and clear, and Collingwood's XI contained seven state players. "You can bat, Jack," said Stackpole triumphantly. "Next fucking week." In fact, Melbourne batted that day. In 53 deliveries, Iverson claimed seven wickets for six runs, including a spell of six for one. Collingwood crumbled for 94.

The circumstances were repeated in Iverson's first Shield outing at the WACA. After claiming six West Australian wickets for 47 in the first innings, he absorbed some punishment from Wally Driver in the second and came up with two for 136. Colin McDonald remembers Iverson drooping in the dressing room afterwards. "I can't cope with this," Iverson said. "I'm a failure." Again, however, redemptive success was at hand: four days later in Adelaide, he took seven South Australian wickets for 77.

Not that there was anything dislikeable about Iverson, says McDonald. He simply didn't realise how good he was:

Jake had a bit of an inferiority complex when it came to other cricketers. He'd never been through the rough and tumble, never understood that some days are good and some are bad, because it had never been hard for him.

For all his varying humours, too, here was a spinner *sui generis* who would surely test English mettle in the forthcoming Ashes series. *Sporting Life* introduced him to the wider public as "Wrong Grip Jake" through a long Whitington profile and a series of "magic eye" photographs. Such was the publicity that, when Freddie Brown's Englishmen arrived in Melbourne to play Victoria in November 1950, Len Hutton made a beeline for Iverson at their Windsor Hotel reception. "I don't suppose," the Yorkshireman said wryly, "that you'd like to show me how you hold the ball." Iverson kept his hand round his glass.

In fact, Iverson began nervously in the tour match, conceding 12 in his first over. Soon enough, though, he was posing the same sort of perplexities as Sonny Ramadhin had posed in England four months earlier. Denis Compton was defeated by his first three deliveries, surviving a stumping only when the ball became marooned in Ian McDonald's pads. "I have never seen him (Compton) so befuddled by any bowler," decided Jack Fingleton.

Iverson's Australian selection was now almost preordained and, despite unsympathetic conditions in Brisbane, he finished off the first Test with four for 43. He then reached his zenith on 9 January 1951, the last day of the third Test at the SCG, where he conceded only 27 runs from 158 deliveries and accumulated six wickets: Hutton, Washbrook, Simpson, Brown, Bedser, Warr. When the delivery that reclaimed the Ashes ran from Warr's stumps to Keith Miller at slip, Iverson confided: "I wouldn't mind a piece of that." Miller replied: "You'll get it, son." The ball was mounted by the NSW Cricket Association for presentation. Iverson, Fingleton said, "bowled as well on this day as I have seen an Australian spinner bowl". What a pity, added Bill O'Reilly, that his career would likely be brief.

Had he come to the game with all his present ability as a young man, he would most assuredly have become one of the great bowlers of all time. He has those attributes, length, control and vicious spin, which consistently pay the highest dividends in international cricket.

A physician noticed he was "withdrawn, reserved and remote". Dr Seal recommended **electro-convulsive therapy**

On an easy pitch not kindly to spin he bowls accurately enough to command constant respect, but on one such as this last day in Sydney he becomes a first-class matchwinner.

For a month or so, Iverson was the toast of Australian cricket. He performed his repertoire for Cinesound at the home ground of his original Brighton club, the newsreel camera positioned behind the batsman's stumps, a small but appreciative crowd behind the bowler's arm.

Almost half a century later, the footage is quite mesmerising: the toppie skids through, the leggie turns just enough, the wrong 'un breaks quite massively. And as though to deepen the mystery, the hand is obscured by a black square so that its varying attitudes cannot be associated with individual deliveries. Iverson does not speak, and barely acknowledges the camera. Shyly but intently, he spring-loads a ball in his fingers and squeezes it out a couple of times. The ball whirrs, even seems to hover, before settling back in that huge hand. It is like a magician producing a dove from his shirt cuff.

Historian Alf Batchelder recalls watching the film at St Kilda's Palais Theatre. As a wheeze, management invited Iverson on stage to demonstrate his bowling to a juvenile batsman protecting a box. The tennis ball bounced once one way, then another, past the probing boy and into the ersatz wicket. For more than 40 years, Batchelder doubted the evidence of his own eyes, until he interviewed Jean Iverson while compiling an entry on her husband for the *Oxford Companion to Australian Cricket*.

Yes, she said matter-of-factly, her husband could do that. That and so much else.

THE MIRACLE OF IVERSON, however, was even now almost over. A veritable Bletchley Park of batsmen had been working on his Enigma code and, if they never quite obtained verbatim translation, had picked up sufficient of a gist to jam his frequency.

Arthur Morris and Miller had twigged that Iverson could be picked in the air: the high-tossed ball tended to be the top-spinner, the lower-trajectory delivery the wrong 'un. In a Shield match at the SCG three weeks after Iverson's Test heroics there, Morris and Miller pillaged him for more than five an over. Morris, who'd scored 29 in his four preceding innings, made 182, and followed it with 206 in the fourth Test at Adelaide Oval a week later. Iverson bowled only modestly in the first innings of the same match and, when he crooked an ankle bowling in the nets before the final day's play, did not bowl in the second.

Unable to trust the joint in the fifth Test, Iverson was still less effective, and surgery was eventually necessary to repair a chip of bone. Hutton was by now also giving signs of having penetrated the mystery, sensing with Yorkshire pragmatism that Iverson's leg-break hardly turned and that the main threat was the occasional straight one. Ian McDonald remembers the confusion that this caused Iverson:

"Hutton actually said it within my hearing: 'I play Iverson as an off-spinner.' Which is basically what he was, though he was a very good one, Jim Laker-class. But it worried Jack. He started saying: 'Everybody knows I just bowl wrong-uns. I've got to start bowling more leg-spinners.'"

So he started to change his bowling round completely, bowling almost all leg-breaks with only a few wrong 'uns thrown in. But he wasn't any good that way, wasn't half the bowler.

Iverson succeeded for Melbourne in his new vein in 1951-52, taking 36 wickets at nine apiece. But he played only one unrewarding Shield game against Queensland over Christmas 1951 before absenting himself for the rest of the season, citing pressures of work with his father's estate agency, H W Iverson of 405 Collins Street.

There were high hopes of what Iverson might achieve in England on the forthcoming Ashes tour. Clive Fairbairn remembers the opinion of the sagely Bill Ponsford:

A lot of us at the time reckoned that Bill was the best judge of cricket and cricketers around. So I used to go see him a bit, have a cup of tea with him, wrack his brains. And one day I asked him: "What do ya reckon the big bloke'd do in England?" Bill says: "Under a good captain, he'd rewrite the record books."

Iverson began the 1952-53 season with three for 38 against South

Africa, then four for 65 against South Australia. But he was freely expressing dissatisfaction with his form, and took umbrage at the laughter that followed one characteristic fielding effort in Adelaide that saw him allow five at deep fine-leg. The annual derby against NSW in Melbourne was three days away, and shaped as Iverson's acid test, but he did not sit it. Teammate George Thoms remembers the Adelaide-Melbourne train journey:

"I was sharing a sleeper with Jake, and he didn't say a word the whole trip home. Next day I opened the paper and there was Jake saying that he wasn't available to play against NSW, and for the rest of the season, because of his work."

Thoms also had an indication of the pressure under which Iverson now found himself when he had a drink during the game with the combative New South Welshman Sid Barnes. "I see Iverson pulled out," Barnes said. "We were going to fix him right up." For his own part, Iverson told *Sun News-Pictorial* journalist Rex Pullen: "I've bowled badly for Victoria this season. I feel it's better to do the right thing and be honest with myself and Victoria's team than to play on and perhaps be dropped."

It was not quite the end for the chimeric Iverson. He claimed 33 wickets at 6.6 for Melbourne in 1953-54, and spent five weeks in India with a Commonwealth side taking 27 wickets at 22 in six matches, including one at Eden Gardens caught by Sam Loxton from an underarm delivery:

I was standing at silly mid-on. I saw this fella miss the first six from Jake, then the second six, and Jake says: "Mr Umpire, I propose to bowl the ball underarm." Oh, the umpire's face was a sight to behold. I thought: "This I gotta see." Anyway, it floats down and the guy's mesmerised. He pushes forward, straight into my hands, and I caught it and put it in my pocket.

It was a suitable coda to one of cricket's craziest melodies. It seems inconceivable that someone whose 157 first-class wickets cost less than 20, his 21 Test wickets barely 15, should desert the game. But then, Jack Iverson had barely been conceivable in the first place.

ONE IS CONSCIOUS in writing of Iverson well after the fact that memories are recomposed by subsequent events. When a man takes his own life, all recollections of him tend to be seasoned by that single fact. Those that might have hinted at future conduct are preserved, those that do not seem to fit overlooked.

The fact is that Iverson, however fragile his confidence on the field, coped rather better with retirement than many cricketers. He began commentating for the ABC in 1954, first on radio then television. He bought a house in Brighton's Black Street in 1956, and raised two daughters with his wife. He joined the Brighton Hospital committee and, in June 1960, took over his father's estate agency completely, renaming it J B Iverson Pty Ltd. For the Real Estate Registrar, neighbour J Lloyd Jones wrote him a number of fulsome references. One from 1962 reads:

I have found him of unimpeachable character, scrupulously honest, temperate and of the strictest moral integrity. His career as an international cricketer proclaims his ready ability to accept without question the vicissitudes of sport and this same ability is amply evidenced throughout his business transactions.

The management of (ABC TV) ABV-2, in selecting and engaging John Iverson as sporting commentator, must necessarily have been impressed by his impartial attitude toward opposing parties...The highest tribute I can pay him is to state that, when our dividing fence was recently renewed, it included at my suggestion a party gate (without bolts or locks) so that each of us, as well as members of our families, might be have free access to the rear garden of the other.

Iverson even revisited cricket for a season or two, underwriting another Brighton premiership in 1961-62 with 70 wickets at 8.9 aged 46.

In August 1963, however, J B Iverson Pty Ltd suffered the unexpected death of its most valued employee, office manager Barry Rea. Replacements did not work out and, in a deposition later placed before coroner Harry Pascoe, Jean Iverson expressed the view that her husband began taking on too much work:

The New Ball

Business pressure was building up considerably. He was trying so hard to get established in the business that I believe it started to affect his health... He was a person who worried over small things but, as he went on, these mounted up and he felt he could not cope.

Jean Iverson became worried about her husband's health around October 1965 and subsequently took him to their family doctor, Dr Alan Callister of the New Street Clinic. A mild stroke was diagnosed, three weeks' bed rest prescribed, but Iverson was still unwell when he returned to work and beginning to act "very strangely". He was examined by a Collins Street physician, who found no sign of disease but noticed he was "withdrawn, reserved and remote". In four consultations with a South Yarra psychiatrist, he was also unresponsive.

In 1968, Iverson was referred to Dr Eric Seal, a neuro-psychiatrist in charge of the St Vincent's Psychiatric Clinic. Seal suspected cerebral arteriosclerosis – a narrowing of the vessels to the brain that, like a chemical imbalance, can cause depression – and recommended a course of electro-convulsive therapy. Once a month for the next three years, Jean Iverson took her husband to Moreland's Sacred Heart Hospital. She recalled:

He was right one day but the next day he would be sick again. There was a period where I noticed he was losing coordination. His speech was slurred and he had trouble sleeping. He would take many anti-depressant tablets...He got upset very easily and on some days he looked shocking. His face and hands were a horrible grey.

Making matters worse, both Iverson's parents died within a year. Indeed, the only times his condition seemed to lift were when he visited Queensland in December 1971 and July 1973. He responded to the warm weather, played golf, talked about moving there. Returning to Melbourne after the second trip, he told friends he intended selling up and shifting to Caloundra. One day, Clive Fairbairn returned to his sports store in Little Bourke Street to be told by his assistant John Scholes (the Victorian batsman): "Big Ivo's been looking for you. Reckons he's gonna move to the Sunshine Coast, play a bit of golf, go fishing, do a bit of swimming." Fairbairn laughed loudly: "He's got the job I'm after."

The process of selling house and business, though, was protracted. Iverson's mood swings became more pronounced, his wife commenting: "Jack was a person who went very much within himself. There were many periods when he couldn't communicate with anyone and there were periods of blankness."

When Seal saw him last on 22 October, he told the coroner, Iverson seemed "fit, well and cheerful". But the following afternoon, Jean Iverson found her husband sitting in the living room with his face and hands "that horrible grey colour" and "upset and shaking visibly". He was hurt and affronted that the buyer of his business was disputing Iverson's legal entitlement to commissions on three properties and insisting on their deduction from the purchase price. Jean Iverson tried to console him and thought she had succeeded, so did not worry at first when he vanished out the door into his shed. By the time she investigated, it was too late.

ON THE FACE OF IT, I could now answer Bill Brown's question. Iverson fitted one of suicide's so-called classic causes: financial anxiety. Yet, as A Alvarez wrote in his classic study of suicide, *The Savage God*:

A suicide's excuses are mostly by the way...They are like the trivial border incident which triggers off a major war. The real motives... belong to the internal world, devious, contradictory, labyrinthine, and mostly out of sight.

Therein, perhaps, lies the lesson in the life and death of Jack Iverson. More than 2,000 men have played cricket for their countries, and what have we really known about any of them? Even today, when we study and write about players so exhaustively, the idea that we can obtain a measure of their character is essentially a journalistic vanity. No-one who watched or wrote about Jack Iverson can have had any concept of his frail sporting self-worth. No-one who played with him could fathom the depths of his disappointments and fears. By a man's cricketing deeds, we can know only the merest fraction of him. 🄌

Michael Atherton Old Trafford, June 1997

STEVE WAUGH ADELAIDE, JANUARY 1994

Barton Funk
The Wrong'Un

Barton Funk is a former tram driver turned poet with an unhealthy obsession for the films of the Coen Brothers, an even unhealthier infatuation for Danny La Rue, and an MA in applied logic from the University of Life (those cheating allegations, he insists, were never substantiated). He is currently seeking a publisher for his first collection of verse, *In Praise of Declaration Bowling.*

Favourite Ashes innings
Chris Old's 29 at Headingley in 1981, the quintessential neglected masterpiece. Without it, Botham and Willis would have performed their heroics in vain.

England keep losing because... they lack the innate motivation of their Commonwealth kith and kin. Turn Tests into all-club affairs and watch 'em go.

"'Ow the 'ell are yer, yer old wanker." Humphrey 123 enunciated the words with excruciating deliberation. That high-pitched drawl made him sound uncomfortably like Dame Edna Everage after availing herself of one too many free samples on a guided tour of a helium factory. While Dick Van Dyke may have enjoyed a lengthy and untroubled reign as the world's most ludicrous Cockney, Humphrey had just usurped Meryl Streep as the planet's least credible Cobber.

"What's a wanker?" queried Jason 11021, brushing a pomegranate seed off his freshly-laundered, eco-friendly, duck-down-flavoured polystyrene pillow. He knew perfectly well what it was. A battered bootleg copy of the 1999 Oxford Dictionary had been doing the rounds at school and he'd snagged two full hours on the loo with it. All the same, there was nothing that titivated him more than seeing Humphrey squirm.

"Ummm, weeell..." began Humphrey, stalling frantically. Moments like this provided a distressing reminder that he was, lest he dare forget, a great-grandfather. As a mere stripling of 76, there were only 65 years between him and the boy-man trying valiantly to fake an interest in his bedtime story. It felt more like a lifetime. IQ of 196 or no, this lad had no concept whatsoever of the vast majority of things he held dearest: the County Championship and Radio 2; free voting; the English National Party; broadsheet newspapers sans Page 15 Android; electric lawnmowers; live music and cinemas with more than 20 seats; foul Februarys and morose Marches; laundrettes; otters; non-organic roast boar. And masturbation. Which had been banned by the Holy Microsoft Emperor in 2019, on the somewhat dubious grounds that wasted semen was damaging the ozone layer, not to mention population growth. Armed resistance in User Sector England had only lasted a couple of hours.

"Put it this way. It's not a compliment. Anyway, if I may continue." Humphrey was in one of his crotchety moods, albeit with good reason. He'd just lost his contract as a hard disc massager, the Stock Market had crashed for the third time that week and, to cap it all, User Sector Europe had just lost its 15th Ashes series in a row. In the wake of a top-order collapse on the sixth day of the fifth Test at the Prague Microsoft SuperDuperDome, not even a record last-wicket stand of 223 between Wilfred Strassen and Jorge Hurstacio could stave off a 17th consecutive innings defeat.

"Continue, I beseech thee," urged Jason, straining his utmost to stifle a yawn and failing miserably.

Humphrey cleared his throat with a theatrical flourish. " ' 'Ow the 'ell are yer, yer old wanker,' said the voice on the other end of the videophone. Dick was speechless. Only one person in the world had ever addressed him in such a disrespectful manner, but he hadn't had seen hide nor hair of Rick Turpin since...well, since that unfortunate business with the chairman of selectors' daughter, which was all of, what, 25 years ago? Besides, Rick didn't have an Aussie accent. And he certainly didn't have a nose quite as unsightly as that. And he'd definitely never have been seen dead or alive with his hair in plaits."

"What's a selector?" enquired Jason, reaching for the buzzer above his bed. Clenching his lips had the desired effect: the smirk did not escape. "Sorry to bother you Robert," he whispered into the intercom, "but I'd be jolly grateful if you could whizz me up a milkshake, preferably guacamole and nutmeg. Promise I'll put some oil on your knee tomorrow."

"Perhaps sir would like an ice-cream fritter to go with that?" offered Humphrey, feeling scant need to disguise his impatience. "And a Non-Diet Extra-Calorific Coke."

"No thanks, great-gramps," smiled Jason, whose perception of sarcasm was a good deal more acute than Humphrey had ever suspected. "But I'll tell you what: I wouldn't half mind a bar of that Galaxy stuff you've been hoarding in your case."

"M-m-my G-g-galaxy!" stammered Humphrey. "Come on, Jason, please, please be reasonable. You know I'd give you a chunk if I could, but I'm down to my last hundred bars. The only thing I value more than real chocolate is my signed scorecard from the Tudor-Stewart Testimonial Match."

"I know, great-gramps, I know," grinned Jason. "Only kidding. Anyway, selectors..."

"Ah yes," continued Humphrey, loosening his favourite paisley cravat, an elderly, unruly little number dotted with ketchup, mustard and sundry other stains of unknown origin. He was what he wore. "The selectors were the chaps who, for a miserly allowance of 300 euros a week, spent their summers in darkened rooms examining videos of every single one of the country's 124 registered professionals and then nominating the eleven least likely to disgrace themselves. Things were so much fairer before Empress Shanette Murdoch brought in all those cloning gurus. Anyway, may we proceed?"

"Proceed, proceed," chuckled Jason, waving his hands in what he hoped was a passable imitation of Marlon Brando. The previous evening, Humphrey had taken him to see *The Godfather* at the local hover-in. Taken aback by the moral ramifications of glorifying a man without a beard, he had zoomed off after the first oxygen break. The guilt had plagued him ever since. To reject one of Humphrey's favourite things was to reject Humphrey.

"We-ell," proceeded Humphrey. "Dick was still figuring out who was on the other end of the line when the voice piped up again. 'You don't recognise me, do you, you old wanker? It's me, Rick. The bloke who sprayed "Graveney's Grave" on the gents door at the Milennium Dome. The bloke who saved your bacon with that stupendous diving catch at midwicket in the national schoolboy trials. The bloke who put cockroach repellent in your sister's peanut butter sandwiches. The bloke who took such inordinate pains to stick each and every page of your dad's 1982 *Wisden* together with Araldite.'

The New Ball

"By now, Dick's head was a fuzzy maze. When his best mate went missing all those years ago, he had led the search, hiring the best private cops money could bribe – besides himself, of course. Dick's real name wasn't Dick, you see. That was just what everybody called him. His real name was Peregrine, so you could understand why he threatened to maim anyone who used it, his mother included.

"Anyway, Dick began to get angry. After two years of schlepping round the world from Venezuela to Vladivostock, he had given Rick up for dead. He even composed the inscription on his virtual tombstone: 'To Rick – Someone Who Could Have Been (And Ruddy Nearly Was)'. He'd taken enormous care over that line, deploying the full breadth of his extensive knowledge of the collected works of Brian Johnston. 'Why the hell didn't you call me before?' he finally blurted. 'I deserved better.'

"Rick swallowed hard. 'Can't explain now,' he whispered conspiratorially. 'Big Sister and all that. But be patient, I'll reveal all. We've got to meet, somewhere discreet. Soon. Nobody else who knew me back then knows I'm alive. Not a soul. The question is: can I rely on you?'

"Dick whistled. Rick expected that. He'd always whistled when he had a tricky decision to make. Tie A Yellow Ribbon Round The Ole Oak Tree if he was merely vexed, I Was Kaiser Bill's Batman if he was sorely troubled. Whistling Jack Smith was never this good."

"Don't worry, great-gramps," butted in Jason, tugging lightly on the sleeve of Humphrey's crumpled PVC blazer. "I remember who Whistling Jack Smith was. The One-Hit Wonders section was the only bit of the Abbey Road Museum I enjoyed. That and the photo of Mike Atherton crooning with Harry Connick Jr at Caesar's Palace."

"Ahem," intoned Humphrey, fearful of losing his thread. Those four vodka-and-broccolis he'd had for supper were beginning to take their toll. "Anyway, as I was saying before I was so heartlessly interrupted, the whistling eventually trailed away. 'OK, OK,' said Dick. 'I can see from my VDU that you're calling from somewhere in suburban Sydney, so you'll have to come here. Just tell me one thing, just to satisfy any mad, lingering doubts that you are who you say you are: name the only man to score a thousand runs in

May and strike an on-drive on to the platform at Warwick Road station.'

"Rick barely drew breath before replying. Dick had been asked that selfsame question by Sir Ray Illingworth during his debut appearance on Anoraks' Roadshow; Channel 222 had covered it live. 'Charlie Hallows,' exulted Rick. 'Good-looking in a sporting sort of way, or so Cardus described him. Right. Old Bull and Bush it is: next Wednesday, twelve-thirty sharp. Be there. Pretty please. For old times' sake.'

"Dick grunted. Rick identified it instantly as a positive grunt. Dick's negative grunts, he recalled, had been much deeper, not to say more prolonged. 'It's The New Bull And Bush now, old man,' said Dick. 'But what the hell. Grab me some duty-free joints, will you? It's still Virgin Tipped. Oh, and a copy of Glenn McGrath's last book if you can find it. Not *Waugh and Peas* but the posthumous one, *Heals And Toes*. Been out of print here for more than 10 years.'

"'Consider it done,' said Rick. He could contain his jubilation no longer. 'I love yer, you old wanker.'

"Dick blushed. 'Oh do shut your cakehole, you soppy old git,' he snapped. Rick smiled sheepishly. 'Y-y-you know something,' he sniffed, struggling in vain to keep the lump in his throat down to manageable proportions. 'I'd k-kill m-my m-mother for a bar of Galaxy.' Dick frowned. 'Now you know I'd do anything for you, old buddy, but let's not push things just yet.'"

Jason's grin would have turned a Cheshire cat green. "So real chocolate was outlawed back then, was it GG?"

"Too right," harrumphed Humphrey. "Thirty-five years ago next Thursday, to be precise. We were going to march on Brussels, yours truly at the head. Some boffin in the Judeo-Christian quarter of eastern Serbia apparently discovered a link between cocoa beans, dried emulsifier and prostate cancer. Never trusted it myself, of course. I always reckoned it was the work of those bastards at Callard and Bowser. They'd have done anything to preserve their market share. Still, they soon got their comeuppance when boiled sweets were outlawed following a landmark case brought by the dentists' union. By the way, I don't care much for this 'GG' business. Great-gramps will do nicely, thank-you."

The New Ball

Jason affected a suitably remorseful expression, pouting for optimum impact. "Sss-orr-eee, great-gramps."

"That's better. Anyway, as I was saying – what was I saying? Ah yes, the meeting at The New Bull And Bush. Rick flew in on schedule and found Dick sitting in a quiet corner by the Digital Karoake machine. Improbable as it seemed, those plaits were even more ridiculous in the flesh. Dick was impressed, nonetheless, by how dapper Rick looked. Nylon boiler-suit, red bandanna, leopardskin brogues. Jeans and tie-dyed t-shirts had been the extent of his wardrobe back in the o-hundreds.

"Instinct had told Dick to buy one of those new-fangled Remote Voice Detectors and turn up at the pub with it fastened behind his right earlobe. He duly made the purchase but that morning he had thought better of it and left it in the basement of his mobile solar pod. How could he betray the man who'd saved him from that pack of irate opposition batsmen at Moreton-in-Marsh? An extensive beating had beckoned that long-ago August afternoon. Fortunately, Rick could have charmed the bullets out of an Uzi. If Tony Blair had possessed even half as silvery a tongue he would surely have won the 2023 Monarchy election playoff, instead of coming a distant third to Ringo Starr and Bill Giles."

Jason startled Humphrey with an elbow to the ribs. "Ringo Who?"

"King Bignose the First to you. The man who turned out to be the creative force behind The Beatles. I'm sure I've told you about them. Tell you what, they had oodles more hits than those undernourished reprobates you keep wittering on about – what do you call them? The Max Bygraves?"

Jason adopted his best laconic sneer, curling his top lip just as he'd practised in front of the bathroom mirror. "The Max Romeos, actually. And yes, of course I've heard of The Beatles. Mum tells me you used to clamp a pair of headphones round her tummy while I was in there, then insist on playing The Continuing Story of Bungalow Bill until I began kicking in protest. Greatest band ever, first to compose a hip-hop waltz in 7/8, last to use non-polyester guitars with real strings, blah, blah, blah. Give me the Bay City Rollers anyday."

Humphrey bristled. "A tad more respect for your elders, if you don't mind, young man. *Anyway*, Dick resolved to keep mum. He bought Rick a pint of virtual real ale then, as the pair clinked glasses, he noticed that the middle joint of the third finger on Rick's left hand was wrapped in what looked remarkably like cotton wool. I say remarkably because, as I'm sure you know, cotton wool had long been declared illegal on account of its use as an aid for blood sniffers, and rightly so." Jason looked sorely insulted.

"'So', said Dick, gesturing towards the misshapen digit, 'half an hour in the country and I see you've managed to break the law already.' Rick feigned innocence. 'What do you mean?' he replied, clearly peeved. 'I've used that stuff throughout my career. Nobody in Asia Sector 3 ever took exception.'

"Dick was stunned. 'What do you mean, "my career"?' he demanded. 'Your so-called career ended before it got out of nappies. That was what all the furore was about, in case you'd forgotten. That's why I haven't seen you for 25 bloody years.'

"Rick brought his left forefinger up to his lips. 'Keep it down will you, old boy. I'll reveal all in good time, but let's go somewhere more private, eh? How about Karl Marx's cemetery? We can check out if that inscription we put on his tombstone is still there. "There's Only One Karl, And Krikken Is His Name" right? And then we can go for a double decaf espresso at that cafe, whatsitsname? Café Haydn... Café Bizet...Café Mozart – yeah, that's it. Café Mozart.'

"Dick bowed his head, shaking it mournfully. 'I'm sorry to have to tell you this, but Cafe Mozart is now an all-night headbanger's disco, but I do know a nice little Angolan diner round the corner. The yamburgers are scrummy. And the pomegranate nut cluster is to die for.'"

Jason playfully slapped Humphrey's left hand. He knew he'd inserted the pomegranate reference purely for his benefit. His addiction was a serious problem, no question about that, what with all the attendant cravings to watch endless footage of Geoff Boycott and Chris Tavaré batting together in India. Still, at least those potent seeds had got him through his Six-Plus exams, not to mention the area bowl-off for the Southern Under-Eights. It seemed a small price to pay.

"What's a headbanger, great-gramps?"

The New Ball

"Oh, just some dandruff victims who got their jollies trying to shake out what meagre brains they had freaking out to bands with asinine names like Shallow Mauve and Yellow Sabbath. *Anyway*, so off they went to the cemetery. For a while the silence was unnerving. Dick was bracing himself. What on earth could Rick be referring to? For his part, Rick was mulling over precisely how he should tell his story. How in the name of Good Lord Bill was he going to compress 25 turbulent years into an afternoon chinwag? More to the point, how much could he safely divulge without ruining everything he had worked for over those 25 years?

"Rick broke the uneasy silence. 'Before I can tell you what's been happening to me, I have to know I can trust you completely.' Dick shrugged his middle-order biffer's shoulders, the same rugged shoulders Rick used to stand on to steal those apples from Gubby Allen's garden..."

"Gubby Who?" interrupted Jason, drawing his right wrist up to his mouth to disguise a grin that, unchecked, might conceivably have blinded a goodly chunk of User Sector Scandinavia.

"Oh *do* pay attention, dear boy," scolded Humphrey. "I told you all about Gubby the other day. The Aussie who ran cricket for half a century after putting it about that he refused to bowl Bodyline out of principle, when the truth of the matter was that he was really a double agent. Only the other day I heard somebody extremely well-connected at The Oval confirm that story about him throwing the toss in the fifth Test of '36-37.

"*Anyway*, Dick invited Rick to do his worst, though not before informing him that he had left his Remote Voice Detector at home. He felt that should be proof enough of his loyalty. Rick did not. 'You must understand,' he implored. 'What I'm about to tell you, if disclosed to any third party, even your grandmother, would create so many ripples that the resulting tidal wave could well drown the game altogether. That's why I have to be as sure as I can possibly be that you won't betray me. Which is why I must ask you to swear on the life of CC that you won't breathe so much as a syllable.'"

"CC?" queried Jason, the curiosity for once entirely genuine.

"Why, Christopher Clairmonte, who else?" retorted Humphrey, the tone distinctly aggrieved.

Jason was still none the wiser. "Christopher Clairmonte?" "Christopher Clairmonte Lewis, better known as 'Potty' King Lewie. He'd been an idol to Rick and Dick back at Kilburn Park Primary. To them he was more, much more, than just a mercurial all-rounder with needle-sharp dress-sense, the cheekbones of a Greek god and a complete absence of facial or nasal hair. It wasn't merely that they could recite his analyses innings by innings. CC symbolised everything they aspired to: inventive, irreverent, insouciant, inspirational, and, best of all, utterly impervious to the treacherous lure of commonsense. Here was a man who thought nothing of standing at cover in the middle of a Test match and calling his manicurist on his mobile phone, just to check his cuticles were looking sufficiently elegant. To take his name in vain would be a betrayal of all they stood for.

"So Dick paused, then sat down under the one non-soya oak tree left in the cemetery. He couldn't take this lightly. If the story really did turn out to be *that* earth-shattering, he could make a mint selling it to that new satellite TV programme devoted to sporting tittle-tattle, *You've Been Shamed*. Dick's finances were in an awful state; a few million euros would be sufficient to see him through that winter, and the next, and a good few after that. Deciding to give him some time, Rick strolled off on his own. When he returned 10 minutes later Dick was nodding his head gravely and arguing with himself ('What are you doing, Dickbrain?...Being a mate, you tosspot').

"'What's up?' asked Rick as he sat down beside him. 'Nothing much,' shrugged Dick. 'Just that I've decided to do your bidding, even if it does mean denying my wife and kids their inalienable right to eat caviar with their chips for the next couple of years.'

"Rick smiled softly. 'Right, let's get cracking then. I s'pose I ought to start from the beginning.'

"Might not be a bad idea,' said Dick gruffly, grabbing a handful of damp leaves and taking some enormous gulps. 'Don't you miss the smell of real leaves?'

"'Let's go back to O-Three,' proposed Rick. 'A largely unredeemable year for English cricket, you may recall. The Saudis trounced us in the World Cup semis, the Sri Lankans won all three Tests here, only Sheffield and London A saw fit to cap a player, five

The New Ball

of the first six batsmen in the national averages were Belgians, and that prize pranny NCTJ Alexander broke all first-class records with 35 consecutive maidens while playing for the Wimps against the Lads in the Phil Tufnell Memorial Match at Shenley.'"

Jason could contain his giggling no longer. He hadn't the foggiest who NCTJ Alexander was, still less cared, but boy, did he love that word "pranny". For sheer onomatopoeic splendour it was almost up there with his all-time favourite Humphreysim, "nincompoop".

"*Any*-way," continued Humphrey tetchily. "Where was I?"

"Prannying on about something highly irrelevant that happened a long time ago, I believe."

"Ah yes," said Humphrey. 'Anyway,' said Rick. 'You may recall that that was also the summer you coaxed me into dating Zoe, PBH's daughter by his secret second marriage. You thought it was quite a clever move for a left-arm googly bowler from a secondary modern, didn't you? Well, it didn't pan out quite as you or anyone else pictured. True, we did have a row at Stringfellow's that night. And yes, I did shove a grapefruit in her face. But PBH's chums in the media bribed me to keep quiet about what really ensued. Paid me handsomely, too. Enough to start a new life.'

"'C'mon, pressed Dick. 'Cut to the coppin' chase.'"

Jason was lost again. More significantly, he was now hearing two words in every three. Indifference had melted. He was hooked. That said, how could he possibly resist such a glaring opportunity to wind Humphrey up? "What's coppin'?"

"Short for copulating. An oath, a swear word, invented by Freddie Flintoff if I'm not mistaken. Then again, the wonders of a good oath are something to which your generation of agnostic aetheists are sadly oblivious. Can't remember the last time I heard you or any of your chums say 'blimey' or 'damn'. It's a disgrace. A chap needs to let off steam. Which was why copulating itself – or squishing, as your generation so inelegantly re-phrased it – was so necessary back then. I acknowledge that the Orgasmatron has benefited mankind immensely, but I still think there's something to be said for actually touching someone else's flesh."

"C'mon, GG," smirked Jason. "Cut to the coppin' chase."

Humphrey scowled. "*Anyway*. So Rick began to explain. 'The

official ICC website, as you will remember, put out a story saying some up-and-coming spinner had raped Zoe and, as a consequence, my three-week contract with Wessex would be "re-categorised" forthwith. I couldn't let on to anyone . Not even my three shrinks. But I thought you'd realise the truth, after all we'd been through together. That I was utterly incapable of exchanging bodily fluids with a member of another gender. What hurt was that you chose to believe the Web rather than trust me.'

"Dick's eyebrows were now hopelessly knotted. 'Hang. On. A. Mo," he intoned, the hesitant, staccato rhythm amplifying his cluelessness. 'I never suspected for a nano-second that you were of the faith. I thought you played along for my sake, coming along to all those Elton John gigs and screaming for a lock of his hair. I put all my energies into making sure you made it. I knew I couldn't, not given my, er, persuasion.'

"Rick smiled wanly. 'And I couldn't tell you, because I knew if it ever slipped out I wouldn't stand a chance. The simple facts of the matter were that Zoe tried to seduce me, whereupon, in a fit of pique brought on by a sudden overwhelming sense of the hypocrisy of it all, I told her I didn't bowl that side of the stumps. Which is why she jabbed that cocktail stick through my finger, and why I responded with that grapefruit. I used to worship Cagney.'

"Cagney?" interjected Jason. "As in Cagney and Lacey, right?"

"No, as in Cagney and Bogey. *Angels With Dirty Faces*, Look Ma, Top o' the World. Isn't one of your modules this term Hollywood and Pinewood Studies or something?"

"Existential Motifs in Anglo-American Televisual Art 1980-2020, actually," corrected Jason, "but do go on."

"WE-LLLLL-UH," harrumphed Humphrey, now fast approaching complete exasperation. His complexion was redder than a blushing Commie pinko with a severe dose of scarlet fever. Jason expected those veins throbbing in his temple to burst at any moment.

"Well, as I was saying. So Rick decided to come clean – lock, stock and smoking barrels. 'First,' he began, taking a deep breath, 'Vanessa Redgrave, who'd just succeeded that Posh Spice thingie as First Lady to President Cleese, personally hurried my papers through the appropriate channels. She'd tipped off the Antipodean Cricket

The New Ball

Board about how I might well be the answer to their prayers. After that shock loss of the Ashes the previous winter and the simultaneous retirement of Shane Warne, they were game for anything.

"'Cue an intensive eight-month course of re-education by hypnotherapy: by the end I could sing Tie Me Kangaroo Down Sport backwards. I could even spell Woolloongabba. Then came the plastic surgery. Nobody could ever recognise me. What I asked for was a cross between Mel Gibson and Mel Brooks but, as you can see, I wound up as a cross between Mel Torme and Heidi. I'm still not absolutely positive the gain was worth the pain.

"'For 10 years I was supposed to lie low, so they fixed me up as a door-to-door Vegemite salesman. Home was a bedsit in Wagga Wagga. After that, though, I was cleared to play again. I went to Canberra and the President himself assured me he would do everything in his power to ensure I was given a fair crack of the whip. What a bloke! He even passed the Anti-Gay-Bashing Bill, the first such legislation anywhere in the northern universe. At last, I was free, free to be myself, free to resume my quest without fear of getting my nasal membranes reassembled, as the lads so exquisitely put it. Australia – sorry, User Sector Asia 3 – has seemed so much more enlightened since they elected Merv Hughes.'"

"It wasn't Merv Hughes at all," scoffed Jason. "Didn't it subsequently emerge that he was a Maori who'd undergone some new-fangled skin-tinting operation?"

"Look," barked Humphrey, lowering his X-ray spectacles in the manner much beloved by viewers of his first and last TV game show, *What's My Fetish?* "We didn't know anything about that at the time. Indulge an old man just this once, eh?"

"Anything you say," said Jason distractedly as Robert finally clunked and whirred his way into the tent, guacamole and nutmeg milkshake perched precariously on the retractable ledge below his chin. "Sorry sir," said the Inanimate Domestic Assistant nervily. "Cock-up on efficiency front. Faxing guacomole not as straightforward as Robert imagined." Jason glanced at that shiny brow. Were those beads of sweat trickling down or was the avocado hair dye running again? "That's OK, Robert, better late than early, as the actress said to the train driver. Now what was that about nasal membranes, GG?"

"So Rick told Dick how he started having nets at St Kilda," resumed Humphrey, steadfastly ignoring the provocation. 'They even brought along Johnny Gleeson to show me how he perfected his flick with the folded second finger,' enthused Rick. 'I was so flattered. And pretty soon, hey presto, I'd perfected a new delivery of my own. Using my third finger in conjunction with my thumb I found I could spin the ball anti-clockwise, which was unheard of at the time. If delivered round-arm, I found I could get such purchase that the ball would pitch leg, nip away towards off, then zip back to leg. Sounds impossible, I realise, but I swear on CC. It's amazing what you can do with strong fingers and long nails.

"'You always did have such sturdy hands,' vouchsafed Dick admiringly, now staring at his rediscovered buddy with the gooiest goo-goo eyes seen outside a bedroom since King Kong fell for Fay Wray. 'Elegant but sturdy.'

"'Called it the Johnny Rotten,' said Rick proudly, too preoccupied to detect this new agenda. 'It kept coming back. Mind you, nobody outside the St Kilda first-team squad knew anything about it, because of the risk of you Poms finding out. For three years I was the best-kept secret this side of the Windsor corgi experiments. I was being groomed. I even had to change my identity for Grade matches, just so suspicions wouldn't be alerted.'

"'What about the opposition?' asked Dick. 'Surely they must have spotted something odd just by watching your hand?' Rick winked. 'That was the ingenious part of it,' he boasted. 'I grew this really shaggy beard and buried my hands in it as I came in. Imagine a rabbi in whites and you'll get the general picture. My arm action was so quick nobody could ever get a proper look at my grip. Admittedly, I copied Paul Adams, only in my case, as one of my wittier teammates put it, I wasn't so much a frog in a blender as a toad in a spin-dryer.'"

"Ah, a spin-dryer," snickered Jason. "Isn't that where the Anglo-Franco Cricket And Darts Board used to send alcoholic slow bowlers?" Humphrey harrumphed, then bit his lip while checking his turbo-charged blood pressure wrist monitor. He was not to be deterred. The finishing post was in sight. Besides, Jason's eyelids were displaying encouraging signs of drooping.

The New Ball

"ANY-way. Rick was just getting to the crunch. 'It was all planned in the minutest detail,' he went on, 'nothing left to chance. I would appear in one series, suffer a stroke at the victory party then retire to a seven-figure pension and a five-storey mock-Georgian pod in Paddington. Everything was in place by the time the 2018 series rolled around.

"'I was hauled before the Sydney media a fortnight before the tourists arrived on the new Indian Ocean rail link. I was presented as a veteran of bush cricket who'd spent the previous decade working with Aboriginal children while developing a unique, highly unorthodox delivery that would bamboozle the Poms. You can imagine the stir. I only made one appearance in the Max Walker Shield but match figures of 15 for 38 were enough to convince the doubters. Inflicting a pair on the Test skipper, "Kaiser" Bill Broonzy, didn't hurt either, I can tell you.'

"Dick's jaw dropped. Rick noticed that his tonsils were still intact. At last, the fog had lifted. Silence reigned momentarily, whereupon the pair swapped the broadest smirks ever witnessed outside a hyena convention. 'I think I can fill in the rest, thanks,' chirped Dick sardonically. "Fifty-two wickets in the rubber at five-point-three apiece. First to take 10 wickets in five consecutive Tests. Bowled Ranjesh Patel between his knees three innings running. You're coppin' Robin Lachmann, you coppin' traitor.'"

Humphrey sighed, stretched his arms and repaired to the illegal IBM Bournvita 'n' Bourbon dispenser behind the tent flap. Jason was the first Englishman to hear his tale. And heaven knows he'd been tempted. Life hadn't been easy, what with the three divorces and those 20 interminable years at that accursed widget factory. He felt dizzy, light-headed, unburdened. Jason ferreted out the last dregs of guacamole and yawned.

"I suppose you know what all this means, GG," he sniggered. "Your mate Rick was Kaiser Bill's Robin." ◗